I AM

The Soul's Heartbeat

Volume 1

The Seven I AM Sayings in the Gospel of St John

Kristina Kaine

I AM The Soul's Heartbeat Volume 1
The Seven I AM Sayings in the Gospel of St John
First Published as a weekly Newsletter in 2003
Second Edition published as Kindle ebook in December 2012.
This Print version published in March 2013

This book is written from the insight of the author, if similar information is found in other books this is co-incidental. Quotes by other authors are referenced.

More information about the author's websites is listed at the end of this book.

Cover design: Adriana Koulias

Cover artwork: Alba Madonna by Raphael

Published by
I AM Press
ISBN: 0975008331

ISBN-13:9780975008331

DEDICATION

This book is dedicated to you.
May each one who reads this book discover the jewel hidden
within your soul.

.

CONTENTS

ACKNOWLEDGMENTS

Thank you to all those who encourage me to write. Thank you to all those who read what I write. Thank you to all those who have proofread what I write.

.

Kristina Kaine is one of the most profound thinkers of our age. She has digested the thinking of great initiates like Rudolf Steiner and reworked their insights into marvelous revelations to us. I strongly recommend her book to anyone who is the least bit curious about how we Human Beings relate to the Cosmos and how we can better get along in this world today.

Andrew Flaxman
http://www.spiritualsciencebiblestudies

FOREWORD

Beginning on New Year's day in 2003 I first began writing about alternative meanings of The Bible. I reflected on the seven I AM sayings in the Gospel of St John which were read each Wednesday when a few of us gathered together to share bread and wine. As the year progressed more people asked to receive the reflections by email, including people interstate and overseas. Their encouragement inspired me.

My words are influenced by my spiritual mentor Rev Mario Schoenmaker (1929-1997) who for 14 years filled me with a new way to read the mystery teachings in the Bible. He would say that all the different interpreters and translators who interfered with the Bible down the centuries could never destroy its secret and eternal meaning – they simply revealed their own level of understanding. This work is dedicated to him, in deep gratitude and respect.

The idea of focusing on these I AM sayings was conceived while reading the works of Friedrich Rittelmeyer, specifically *Meditation – Guidance of the Inner Life*. You will find his ideas woven within my words and occasionally quoted. Inspiration has also come from conversations with my friends as well as study of other esoteric teachers including Rudolf Steiner and his pupils, as well as Corinne Heline and others. As reflections they were inevitably influenced by what was going on in the world at the time, notably the 2003 Gulf War.

Where I have based a whole reflection on an article or lecture by another person, or have used direct quotes, I have stated so; the rest is the result of my own personal reflection. Deep gratitude also to my friend Patricia Clarke (1953 – 2005) for not only bringing me into the orbit of Rev Mario Schoenmaker on 28 October 1982, but also for her generous assistance with graphics, layout and printing in many areas of my life.

These individual Reflections can be used for meditation and contemplation. My hope is that all who read and contemplate them will find the spirit of Christ woven through the words.

Michaelmas 28 September 2003

THE BIBLE TEXTS OF THE I AM SAYINGS

Revised Standard Version

I am the Bread of Life

Jesus said to them, "I am the bread of life; he who comes to me shall not hunger, and he who believes in me shall never thirst." John 6:35

I am the Light of the World

Again Jesus spoke to them, saying, "I am the light of the world; he who follows me will not walk in darkness, but will have the light of life." John 8:12

I am the Door of the Sheep

So Jesus again said to them, "Truly, truly, I say to you, I am the door of the sheep. All who came before me are thieves and robbers; but the sheep did not heed them. I am the door; if any one enters by me, he will be saved, and will go in and out and find pasture. The thief comes only to steal and kill and destroy; I came that they may have life, and have it abundantly." John 10:7

3

I am the Good Shepherd

"I am the good shepherd. The good shepherd lays down his life for the sheep. He who is a hireling and not a shepherd, whose own the sheep are not, sees the wolf coming and leaves the sheep and flees; and the wolf snatches them and scatters them. He flees because he is a hireling and cares nothing for the sheep. I am the good shepherd; I know my own and my own know me, as the Father knows me and I know the Father; and I lay down my life for the sheep. And I have other sheep, which are not of this fold; I must bring them also, and they will heed my voice. So there shall be one flock, one shepherd. For this reason the Father loves me, because I lay down my life, that I may take it again. No one takes it from me, but I lay it down of my own accord. I have power to lay it down, and I have power to take it again; this charge I have received from my Father." John 10:11

I am the Resurrection and the Life

Jesus said to her, "I am the resurrection and the life; he who believes in me, though he die, yet shall he live, and whoever lives and believes in me shall never die. Do you believe this?" John 11:25

I am the Way, the Truth and the Life

Jesus said to him, "I am the way, and the truth, and the life; no one comes to the Father, but by me. If you had known me, you would have known my Father also; henceforth you know him and have seen him." John 14:6

I am the True Vine

"I am the true vine, and my Father is the vinedresser. Every branch of mine that bears no fruit, he takes away, and every branch that does bear fruit he prunes, that it may bear more fruit. You are already made clean by the word which I have spoken to you. Abide in me, and I in you. As the branch cannot bear fruit by itself, unless it abides in the vine, neither can you, unless you abide in me. I am the vine, you are the branches. He who abides in me, and I in him, he it is that bears much fruit, for apart from me you can do nothing. If a man does not abide in me, he is cast forth as a branch and withers; and the branches are gathered, thrown into the fire and burned." John 15:1

In the Bible when the Greek words *ego eimi* are used for 'I am' we can read this to mean the fourth member of our being, the I AM. The fourfold human being is comprised of these four elements.

Physical,

Etheric or life forces,

Astral/Soul or consciousness and,

I AM or individuality.

Our present task in evolution is that we become aware of this I AM and more strongly connected with it allowing it to have more influence in all the events of our lives. If we don't, our habitual soul/astral forces often make life difficult by responding to life in a lower, instinctual way.

The seven I AM sayings show how we can develop ourselves to respond to life in the highest way possible.

About the terminology used in these reflections

Esoteric Christianity recognizes the human being as a threefold being of body, soul and spirit. These three can be aligned with the three basic human faculties of will, feeling and thinking in that order.

We have our physical body in common with the mineral kingdom. Our physical body has life because of the presence of a life-force or etheric body. This force is associated with the human drive to survive; to eat, to regulate temperature and comfort, to regenerate and procreate. Humans have this in common with the plant world. An image of the function of the life forces arises when we think of an apple; on the tree it is plump, when left in the fruit bowl it gradually shrivels and rots. This depletion is the result of a waning etheric life-force. If our etheric body fully disconnects from our physical body we die. There are several Greek words in the bible that mean life and refer to our etheric body; *bios, psuche and zoe*. We could say that *bios* is physical life; *psuche* is soul life; and *zoe* is spiritual life. *Soma* is another world that refers to the etheric body. It points to etheric body that has disconnected from the physical which in its highest state is the resurrection body.

Our physical body has movement and experiences emotion because of our astral body or desire body. We have this in common with animals. For instance, plants cannot move around like animals do because they do not have this astral body. We can also call this astral part of us our soul body. If our astral body disconnects from our etheric and physical we become unconscious. In the bible the word *sarx* usually refers to our astral body. The various words for desire point to the lower or higher motives of the astral body; *thelo* – to wish, *epipotheo* - to lust, *epithumia* – to crave or covet, *eudokia* – good pleasure.

The evolving human being refines its astral body through becoming conscious of exactly how they feel, think and will. It is the activity of these three human functions that is actually our soul. The more consciously we use these functions are the more active is our soul. *Psuche* points to the activity of the soul.

When we achieve a certain level of consciousness in our feeling, thinking and will, and only when we do, can we become aware of the human 'I'. Becoming aware of the self in its lowest and highest expressions is, in fact, our life's purpose. When we are not aware of this 'I' component in our being it works in us as a reflection, as a mirrored image. In its lower expression it is egotistical and selfish. This is a necessary part of our development because it makes us aware that we are individuals. Once we experience this selfishness our task is to raise it up to a higher expression. Then we experience ourselves as independent, highly self-aware, individuals. The highest expression of the human 'I' is referred to in the bible as *ego eimi* – I AM. Full awareness of our I AM is to have full self consciousness.

As we become aware of the activity of the 'I' the third part of our being, our spirit, comes to life. This is referred to as *pneuma*. The three activities of our spirit are Imagination, Inspiration and Intuition. We have experiences of these functions when we are able to raise our feeling, thinking and willing to a higher expression through a conscious connection with our 'I'.

The seven I AM sayings show how we can develop ourselves to respond to life in the highest way possible.

1. I AM THE BREAD

One: We must Strive for the I Am

Jesus said to them, "I am the bread of life; he who comes to me shall not hunger, and he who believes in me shall never thirst." Jn 6:35

It is interesting that Jesus makes this statement; not Christ or Christ Jesus or Jesus Christ. St John mostly refers to Jesus and it is staggering how few times the word 'Christ' is mentioned in the Gospel of St John. Only at the end of the second last chapter, in chapter 20, does St John reveal that "Jesus is the Christ" He says:

Now Jesus did many other signs in the presence of the disciples, which are not written in this book; but these are written that you may believe that Jesus is the Christ, the Son of God, and that believing you may have life in his name. Jn 20:30

Perhaps St John did this so that we are able to really identify with Jesus the human being. This is John's way of placing the mighty cosmic mystery firmly into our daily life.

The Gospel of St John can guide us to our higher self, step by step, not in any specific order, so that we can become conscious of higher ways to act in all our daily situations. This is a process of preparing our human being to receive the Christ Impulse that is available to us since Golgotha. The story of a God becoming a man through birth, baptism, crucifixion and resurrection is to become part of our own biography.

As human beings we can then ask: how will the Holy Spirit descend on us so that Christ becomes active in us? How can we can express our I AM as fully as possible within the confines of human evolution? St John reveals the first step to us: "I am the bread of life". He is telling us that the I AM is the bread of life and even though it is our very own personal I AM, we can't have it unless we work for it. We have to 'come' and we have to 'believe'.

'Coming', motion, movement speaks of the work of the I AM in the astral body – that part of our being where motion, emotion and consciousness is centered.

'Believe' is about knowing; knowledge, thinking (not blind belief) is to do with the work of the I AM in the etheric body – the center of our life force which alerts us to hunger and thirst.

So Jesus says that we must act and know, in a bread-of-life way, through the I AM. He is sharing his personal experience with us. He says this must happen in a new way, not through the old patterns that are deeply ingrained in our astral and etheric (for aeons since the previous incarnation of the earth known as Old Moon and Old Sun). This new thing can only happen through our own personal effort where we override our instinctive patterns and allow a new element that is being added in the Earth cycle, the I AM, to influence our astral and etheric bodies.

We have now reached an evolutionary point in time were we are being given direct access of our I AM which has been held in the heavens for us until we 'come of age'. Are we ready? The spiritual hierarchies who are the guardians of our I AM would be thinking: "can we put a 5 year old behind the wheel of a car?" And the thing is that it is no longer up to the hierarchies; the responsibility is now ours! Evolution is at a pivotal point.

And this is where we oscillate and need to call on every ounce of will in our being. There is so much going on within us that is unconscious. Only though our ability to direct our will can we take up the challenge to control our own lives now. One way we can do this is to purposefully contemplate how the I AM could be the *bread of life* that both quells hunger and quenches thirst.

These ideas will only hold meaning for us if we come to know and experience the finer detail of our being. We are beings of body, soul and spirit. Each of these areas can be divided into three parts, each having their own specific function. Our body is formed from what we take into it – what we eat and drink and can be compared to the mineral kingdom. Our etheric body, the life force, maintains the body's shape and produces the drives of survival. It can be compared to the plant kingdom. The astral body gives us consciousness and movement and can be compared to the animal kingdom. Our soul and spirit are the purely human part of our being through which we stand above these other kingdoms and this places us on a different level to animals (something that is not completely understood today). Our I AM is the human element that ennobles us, raising us up to a higher expression, overriding our instincts and unconscious will until be stand with Christ as his co-worker. Through the I AM sayings, St John explains how this is achieved.

◆

Two: Nourish Ourselves with Christened Food

Jesus said to them, "I am the bread of life; he who comes to me shall not hunger, and he who believes in me shall never thirst." John 6:35

One of the keys to this first I AM saying is that the group consciousness of the past is being replaced by a new consciousness of individual responsibility. Much of Chapter 6 compares the past to the future.

When they found him on the other side of the sea, they said to him, "Rabbi, when did you come here?" Jesus answered them, "Truly, truly, I say to you, you seek me, not because you saw signs, but because you ate your fill of the loaves. Do not labor for the food which perishes, but for the food which endures to eternal life, which the Son of man will give to you; for on him has God the Father set his seal." Then they said to him, "What must we do, to be doing the works of God?" Jesus answered them, "This is the work of God, that you believe in him whom he has sent." So they said to him, "Then what sign do you do, that we may see, and believe you? What work do you perform? Our fathers ate the manna in the wilderness; as it is written, 'He gave them bread from heaven to eat'" Jesus then said to them, "Truly, truly, I say to you, it was not Moses who gave you the bread from heaven; my Father gives you the true bread from heaven. For the bread of God is that which comes down from heaven, and gives life to the world." They said to him, "Lord, give us this bread always." Jesus said to them, "I am the bread of life; he who comes to me shall not hunger, and he who believes in me shall never thirst". John 6:25-35

Manna in the wilderness was good enough for our forefathers but it won't work now. Manna from heaven worked then but it won't work now. We must now nourish ourselves through our individual I, we can no longer be nourished by group consciousness.

It is interesting to observe group consciousness. If we ask people how they enjoy spending their time we discover that it is often with workmates and friends, whereas it used to be with family. Or they may say at the pub or a sporting event – these are group conscious substitutes. Careful observation of society reveals that people are afraid to take hold of their own individuality. They just move from one group consciousness to another and pretend that they are expressing their individuality. In fact the governments of the world have labeled these things titty-tainment. A way to keep the masses pacified, breast-fed, so that they don't cause trouble.

Even among those of us who are developing ourselves spiritually we can see the difficultly of expressing our I AM. If we were able to then harmony would prevail. When harmony does not prevail the pseudo I AM, the astral, tries to establish its position; its hallmark is disharmony.

Bread inherently has a self-raising force; yeast that can rise above the simple material elements. Jesus says that the I AM is this bread; the grain, rooted in the earth, growing in the air warmed by the sun, then mixed with water and a raising ingredient. The I AM is this bread of life. He is referring to the highest expression of the I AM, which is Christ as John points out in John 20.

So John is emphasizing that Christ is food and we must feed on him. If we take this bread into us we receive life from it. Unless we give our I AM its rightful place in our being we will always remain hungry. This is the yearning we see all around us. People know that there is manna to be eaten, but they think it will come from heaven, from outside, as a gift. They don't realize that the manna is within them and only through their own effort can they unwrap it and eat it.

The media constantly reminds us that people are overweight, unfit; eating the wrong food amidst a confusion of retracted statements about what is the wrong or right food. Is this a sign of the yearning for this real food? Christ food? Can you imagine going to a restaurant and ordering for a main course "Christ"? … grilled!

This paints a picture of the urgency in the world to realize that Christ is our food, the only food that will satisfy us. We come to the table to eat of him every time we give thanks for the food we eat and every time we prayerfully prepare our food. These are the thoughts that will reveal his presence and his power.

♦

Three: The I and the Anti-I

Jesus said to them, "I am the bread of life; he who comes to me shall not hunger, and he who believes in me shall never thirst. But I said to you that you have seen me and yet do not believe. All that the Father gives me will come to me; and him who comes to me I will not cast out. For I have come down from heaven, not to do my own will, but the will of him who sent me; and this is the will of him who sent me, that I should lose nothing of all that he has given me, but raise it up at the last day. For this is the will of my Father, that every one who sees the Son and believes in him should have eternal life; and I will raise him up at the last day." The Jews then murmured at him, because he said, "I am the bread which came down from heaven." They said, "Is not this Jesus, the son of Joseph, whose father and mother we know? How does he now say, 'I have come down from heaven'?" Jesus answered them, "Do not murmur among yourselves. No one can come to me unless the Father who sent me draws him; and I will raise him up at the last day. It is written in the prophets, 'And they shall all be taught by God.' Every one who has heard and learned from the Father comes to me. Not that any one has seen the Father except him who is from God; he has seen the Father. Truly, truly, I say to you, he who believes has eternal life. I am the bread of life. Your fathers ate the manna in the wilderness, and they died. This is the bread which comes down from heaven, that a man may eat of it and not die. I am the living bread which came down from heaven; if any one eats of this bread, he will live for ever; and the bread which I shall give for the life of the world is my flesh." John 6:35-51

Verse 39 says: *That I should lose nothing of all that he (the Father) has given me, but raise it up at the last day.* When is this 'last day'? Is it some time in the never-never or is it that last day we have just had, that is, yesterday? Have you heard the saying that "today is tomorrow's yesterday, make the most of the present"? So every day will become a yesterday, the last day we just had. This says that we always live in the present and that we must make the most of it; raise it up. The challenge is to engage with the present, not hanker for yesterday or wish it was already tomorrow. The bread of life is in the present. The I AM is the nourisher of the present – The I AM is the bread, the sustenance, of the present.

Yesterday belongs to Lucifer. Tomorrow belongs to Ahriman. Whenever we do not "raise up" our yesterdays, but drag them as-it-was into the present we are the puppet of Lucifer. Whenever we are dissatisfied with today and want to bring on tomorrow, we are the puppet of Ahriman. It takes great concentration, which is the ability to be very conscious, to stay in the present regardless of what is happening there. To do this we need the sustenance of the bread of life, the I AM. When we want to go back to the good old days or you wish today would end, we shut our I AM out.

Now that the Father has given us personal possession of our I AM there is an urgency to have the courage to live in the present. Remember that this 'bread of life' is the central symbol handed down from the last supper – Judas was given the bread along with everyone else. The anti-forces, the anti-I AM, is an integral part of the story. We can learn to deal with these anti-I forces in a cool and collected way so that they can have their rightful place in the present. Or we can get angry with any opposition so that these forces express themselves in the wrong place – the past into the present, or the future wished for too soon - and in that moment we assist the anti-forces to be evil. This is why the great symbol of the sacred meal, the Eucharist, is the bread, the most precious thing on earth for human life. It represents the body, the substance of Christ who is our great I AM.

The day after I wrote this I read the following: "Rudolf Steiner has already shown in his philosophical writings that a world-conception must proceed from the being of man. Not a hypothetical "beginning" (primeval mist etc.), not an abstract principle, but the very last thing that came into being, gives the right starting-point for a knowledge of the universe. In the "Philosophy of Freedom" in Chapter three, there is a passage where Rudolf Steiner points out that to start at the "beginning" is a matter for the world-Creator, but that the seeker of knowledge must start at that which was created last, that is to say: today and here. Carl Unger: *"The Language of the Consciousness Soul"*

◆

Four: The Battle of the I AM

Jesus then said to them, "Truly, truly, I say to you, it was not Moses who gave you the bread from heaven; my Father gives you the true bread from heaven. For the bread of God is that which comes down from heaven, and gives life to the world." They said to him, "Lord, give us this bread always." Jesus said to them, "I am the bread of life; he who comes to me shall not hunger, and he who believes in me shall never thirst. But I said to you that you have seen me and yet do not believe. All that the Father gives me will come to me; and him who comes to me I will not cast out. For I have come down from heaven, not to do my own will, but the will of him who sent me; and this is the will of him who sent me, that I should lose nothing of all that he has given me, but raise it up at the last day. For this is the will of my Father, that every one who sees the Son and believes in him should have eternal life; and I will raise him up at the last day." John 6:32 – 40

The Gospel of St John often speaks to us through what is not said. In the first reflection we saw that the name "Christ" is rarely used, Jesus is called Jesus. Then right at the end in Chapter 20 John says that 'Jesus is the Christ'. We also notice that John never reveals himself as the author, but speaks of himself as 'the Disciple whom Jesus loved'. It is as though after hearing the word 'I' uttered from the mouth of Christ he cannot then use it to refer to himself.

Then in verses 32 to 40 we are drawn by the repeated use of a word like "will" - it appears seven times. The work of the will in our being is unconscious, for instance, we don't know what happens when we digest our food. So why is the will unconscious? Because it has returned with us as an experience from a former life. Whenever we used our will we create a force that will be expressed in the future. According to the extent that we use our will, as well as the caliber of that will, we create forces for our next incarnation.

This shows us how important the will is and it is also why there are so many exercises to develop our will. Reverend Mario Schoenmaker so often emphasized, "Let your 'yes' be 'yes' and your 'no' be 'no'. He knew that the secret of developing our will forces could be found in this activity.

One of the most important will-tasks in this life is to infuse our thinking with will. Not the will that rises up unconsciously from the body, but the force of the will from the Father which is in our I AM. In verse 38 we read, *"For I have come down from heaven, not to do my own will, but the will of him who sent me:"* The will associated with the I AM gives us the ability to control our thinking, to become more aware, more conscious and more aligned with the spiritual worlds.

This first I AM saying gives us clues about how to set this in motion. The I AM is the bread of life, it satisfies hunger and quenches thirst …huh? Since when did we drink bread? Well, hunger and thirst are the organic processes of the body, powerful drives which demand to be satisfied. They are, in fact, the mechanism that attracts the soul to the body; otherwise our soul would prefer to float off into the wide blue yonder with our spirit. The words Christ spoke from the cross, "I thirst" indicate that he was fully incarnated in the body Jesus prepared for him. This was the great Sun Being's first experience of the hidden will forces in the human physical body. This was the signal that he could complete his deed of imbuing the earth and everything in it with love and freedom.

Since Golgotha bread from the bakery will not satisfy our hunger and thirst, only a deepening relationship with our I AM can do that. If we look around in the world we see the substitute for this satisfaction in commercialism and consumerism. People everywhere try to satisfy their growing inner dissatisfaction with outer things.

So we must strive, rigorously strive – which means using the will – to make the strong connection with our I AM, then we shall no longer be dissatisfied, no longer be hungry and thirsty.

So the bread in our passion feast reminds us that the will from the Father is in the I AM and it will give us life.

◆

Five: Letting New Ideas Flow

Jesus said to them, *"I am the bread of life; he who comes to me shall not hunger, and he who believes in me shall never thirst.* John 6:35

If, when we read these bible texts, we can open our imagination new ideas then a new understanding can rise up within us. It isn't about being prescriptive about what the text means but rather it is about the process that happens within our being when a possible meaning comes alive for us. It is like opening a blockage for our energy to flow differently. A simple ideas such as 'last' not meaning the end of time but the last thing we did a moment ago or a day ago can change the whole perspective of a bible text.

By contemplating the ideas that have arisen so far from the statement that 'the I AM is the bread of life' we can each discover even more. For instance, in the last reflection we looked at the idea that our will is unconscious? How does our life change when we realize that we created our will in our last life and that we are presently creating our will for our next life. Do we experience a new level of satisfaction in our life when we observe how bodily desires clamor to be satisfied knowing that they can never be satisfied with worldly things?

In the reflection before that we spoke of how we can drag the past into the present or wish it was tomorrow. Lucifer always wants the good old days and Ahriman wants us to have the future now. How do we find the courage to live in the present with the impulses of the I AM? We need courage because the presence of the I AM in our being creates a pressure that can make us anxious.

In the second reflection we considered the independence of the I AM. Because the I AM is now our personal possession, and personal responsibility, we are freed from group consciousness. But everywhere we look new group consciousnesses arise, at work, through sport, in social gatherings etc. People want their freedom and independence but they can't handle it.

In the first reflection we looked at the clues to finding this bread of life; to 'come' and to 'believe'. We must resist the old patterns of the astral and etheric bodies, created over lifetimes, and let the I AM express itself in us now.

Christ is our food; we must be nourished by him. Christ is the pure cosmic I AM, the bread, that gives us life. It gives us what we require to live and grow and remain healthy; not physically but spiritually.

Two interesting observations about the Gospel of St John were:

One: That the name of Christ is rarely used, it is Jesus who speaks and acts. This helps us to identify with the man which is a much more immediate experience than trying identifying with the God.

Two: That John never reveals himself as the author. After John has heard the word "I" from the mouth of Christ Jesus he cannot bring himself to use it for himself. He can only speak of himself as the Disciple whom Jesus loved. Because he has experienced the reality of the 'I' ahead of most of mankind he feels unworthy to use it. This is his experience of the sacredness of the 'I'.

There can be no doubt that the I AM is a mysterious part of our being. In the 1980s Rev Mario Schoenmaker recommended an exercise for his students. He suggested that we go through a whole day without saying "I" (or me!). This is an excellent thing to do because it draws the force of will into the I AM. It makes us conscious of our place in the world. Our will is the most individual part of us and its destiny is to become free - not free to do what we want but spiritually free. In this process we come to know why we can say, "Not my will but thine".

Rev Mario also said that it was ridiculous to say, "I have a cold, or I have a headache." Your "I" cannot have a cold; it does not experience sickness or death. The I AM is life, the bread of life, the substance or life.

The I AM belongs to eternity because it is the core of the human being that incarnates again and again. The substance of the I AM is love, as we experience our I AM more and more in our daily life so we love more. The pure I AM is perfect love – that is our aim and purpose.

♦

2. I AM THE LIGHT

One: The I AM and Fire

Again Jesus spoke to them, saying, "I am the light of the world; he who follows me will not walk in darkness, but will have the light of life." John 8:12

Light is actually invisible, it makes everything else visible. We don't think about this in our daily life because we are always saying things like, "turn on the light" "shine the light over here" "I need more light". So we talk about light as if it was a thing when really we mean the object that is emitting the light not the light itself.

So the I AM is light – invisible but can make all things visible. Occult knowledge reveals that light is created by fire. The light of the sun is produced by the consuming fire of the sun beings.

Therefore the I AM is created by fire. Fire is warmth so it must follow that when we are warm we have fire within us and that fire creates light. This brings us back to the point that the I AM is light.

So lets look at how we can be warm and light or cold and dark.

- We can look at a flower and see spirit weaving there in the colour, the shape, the smell or we can pass the flower by without noticing it.

- We can be energetic, creative and caring or be a person who couldn't care less about things.

- We can be peaceful, harmonious, cheerful and content or we can allow a bad mood, depression or negativity to overshadow us.

- Then we can see God working in this world, in world events, in the seasons and the religious festivals, or we can not notice these rhythms.

These are the choices we make throughout each day. In freedom we choose to be cold or warm. In the cold, the darkness, the I AM shrinks back and can have no influence. In the warmth the I AM creates a light on our path *"he who follows me will not walk in darkness, but will have the light of life."* Rudolph Steiner saw it this way:

"I gaze into the Darkness.
In it there arises Light —
Living Light!
Who is this Light in the Darkness?
It is I myself in my reality.
This reality of the 'I'
Does not enter into my earthly life.
I am but a picture of it.
But I shall find it again
When with good will for the Spirit
I shall have passed through the Gate of Death."

Entering into meditative words like this we can confront the Darkness. We realize that here on Earth we are only a picture of our true being — that our true being rarely comes down into our earthly life. Yet in the midst of the darkness, through our good will towards the spirit, a light can dawn upon us, of which we may in truth confess: This Light am I myself in my reality."

◆

Two: The I AM Lights the World

Friedrich Rittelmeyer in his book, *"Meditation, guidance of the Inner Life"* suggests that the seven I AM sayings are meditations. This is what he says as he moves from "I Am the Bread" to "I am the Light".

"We can understand, in a living way, that the Mass is not merely about hearing the word, as in the Protestant service, but it is an act in which Christ is the meal – this is a much more powerful experience than hearing words. Christ is the bread, He is proclaimed to us through a meal. The Mass is not only to be heard and to be celebrated, but in all its details it is to be received as a food for the soul.

If in this saying "I am the Bread of life," we have looked down; in the second "I am" we look up. "I am the Light of the world" (John 8, 12). We change our view of the world. It is this spiritual working upon the world that is necessary if man is to become new. To contemplate deeply the words "I am the Light" can build a real temple of light for us. A temple in which we spend our time, retreat to when there is a need. This is not a narrow personal Christianity but a Christianity as great as the world. We can think of all those who have ever worshipped in temples of light. In silent vanished centuries our brothers and sisters have sent up their souls in prayer to the light.

Think of the old Holy Rishis, how they taught their pupils to pray: "We would receive into us the love-awaking light of the great sun-being, which gives life, that it may help our spirit onwards." Think of royal Zarathustra, how he brought to his Persians reverence of the spirit-ruling majesty of the golden sun. We hear the sacred song of the sun echoing from the Egyptian temples in Thebes, in Memphis, in Heliopolis.

We may also think of later times: of how, in the Middle Ages, Francis walked under the glowing sun of Italy:

Praised be Thou, O Lord, with all Thy creatures,
And especially our brother the sun,
He makes the day, and we are lighted by him,
And he is beautiful, and shines with great splendor,
And of Thee O most high he is the symbol.

Think of how in misty Holland, Rembrandt, hungry for light, conceived of his whole art as a feeling after the wonders of light. Think of how, as a priest's service of light, at the summit of German history, Goethe reverently gazed into the "deeds and sorrows of light," of how, in the colors, he recognized the revelation of the Elohim, of how, in his last confession, he reverenced the sun, along with Christ, as the most mighty divine revelation, "which it is granted to us men on earth to see."

Then think of the first divine word of the Bible: "Let there be light," … and of the last one in Revelation about the new world to come: "They need no light of lamp or sun for the Lord God will be their light" (Rev. 22:5.) Between these two statements we can place the words of Christ, "I am the Light of the world." This is a new "Let there be light." But now let it come from within that it may shine through all that is outside. In our meditations seek Christ's being till we experience Him only as light, and penetrate this light until it is Christ Himself. Allow yourself to experience the acts and words of Christ upon earth as if you were there. Experience it as if first-hand. In this way we become light-workers in a higher sphere.

In your meditation see the outward light before you in spirit, as a sea of waves of life, and dive deep into this light as into a healing spring. Feel how your whole being breathes in health in the light. We feel how powers of healing stream forth from the light. Seek to experience Christ in this way. Think not only of His words, but think that the power of healing proceeds from His words, as when the woman became whole by touching the hem of His garment, or the son of the nobleman was healed from a distance. (John 4:51.) Then seek to experience how the light has something still more inward to give our souls. Think about how our souls must be pure if they are to live in light, and how purity flows forth from the worlds of light. This purifying power of light lives in unimagined fullness in Christ. "You are already made clean by the word which I have spoken to you," says Christ to His disciples. That is the healing in the light of Christ. (John 15:3.)

Then listen to the divine harmonies of light, to the deep tranquility and contentment which makes us part of the Divine working. Look from there to Christ as He says, "The peace be with you." The gates of Paradise open through His words, and the harmonies of heaven spread themselves around you. Then see yourself becoming totally light in this light. As in the sunlight, when we give ourselves to it, we seem to become light, through and through, as if we are sunbeams. So fill yourself with divine light from Christ in every corner of your being. Then illuminate, first, your own being with Christ, the Light, then illuminate your environment, then the rest of the world. We are one light with Christ. Look around in this light, try to perceive; even if it is only dimly. Remember, Christ makes the blind see. (John 9:39.) You will begin to experience the food that comes from the sunlight. It is as if a starving man within us had waited for this food of light, as if he wanted to eat his fill at the table of light. And so the light of Christ is food for the light within us. There is a great power that can change the world living in this light, the creative power which speaks at the beginning of the Bible, "Let there be light" can enter into us, we cannot remain the same, we must be changed if we give ourselves up to the power of this light.

Every word we hear from Christ molds us anew. In each word of His there is power, the creative power that existed in the beginning of the world. In each word of His the new man lies dormant, we can awaken that new man.

By deeply contemplating the words, "I am the Light" we are led on a sure path into the world of the "I" which is light, in which the daily sunlight and the highest divine revelation are one in Christ. This is the act of serving God in the temple of the sun.

In the west men have achieved their ego. But there is no light in this ego. In the east men have honored the light. But they have not found their ego in the light. But we are going towards a new world, where we with Christ shall "shine as the same light." "Then shall the righteous shine as the sun in the kingdom of the Father." As Christ says of Himself, "I am the Light of the world" so we can also hear him say to us, "You are the Light of the world!" "

"Meditation, guidance of the Inner Life" by Friedrich Rittelmeyer

♦

Three: The I AM Means Full Self-consciousness

"Again Jesus spoke to them, saying I AM the light of the world; he who follows me will not walk in darkness, but will have the light of life." John 8:12

We have seen how our I AM is a light in the darkness and how we can become, with Christ, the light of the world. The I AM also sheds light on the being referred to as the Father:

The earth exists in order that full self-consciousness, the full expression of the I AM, may be given to mankind. The focal point of the development of the human race is this I AM. Christ is the being who made it possible for every human being – each as an individual – to experience the I AM in themselves.

When we compare the Old and New Testaments we become aware that before Christ fully incarnated, the human being did not yet fully experience the I AM. He experienced himself as a part of a Divine Being just as animals today belong to their group-soul.

A modern Christian – or better put, a Christed person from any religion - feels the presence of the I AM and gradually will learn to experience it more and more. But a Jew from the time of the Old Testament did not feel so enclosed within an individual personality and so could not yet say: "I am an I." Such a person experienced being within the wholeness of the Jewish people and looked up to its group-soul. If they had wanted to express this in words, they would have said: "My consciousness reaches up to the Father of the whole people, to Abraham… I and Father Abraham are one! In my veins flows the same blood that flows in the veins of Abraham."

Then Christ came and he said to his nearest, most intimate initiates: "You have been conscious of being one with God through the flesh, through blood relationships. But you should reach for a still higher spiritual relationship. You should believe in a spiritual Father in which the emerging I AM is rooted, and draw upon a more spiritual substance than the group-soul that binds the Jewish people together. You should believe in what lies within me and within every human being, in what is not only one with Abraham, but also one with the very divine foundation of the world." This is what Christ means when he says: *'Before Father Abraham was, was the I AM!'* He is saying that his I AM not only goes back to the blood-Father, Abraham, but is one with all that flows through the entire cosmos and is beyond religious beliefs. From this height to which his spiritual nature has been lifted he declares: *"I and the Father are one!"* These are important words, which we must experience within ourselves.

How did Christ's initiates respond to his declaration? They said: "No individual physical human being has ever existed before to whom this name of I AM could be applied; Jesus Christ is the first to bring to the world the I AM in its full significance." Therefore, they named Jesus Christ the I AM. That was the name in which they felt themselves united, the name that they understood, the name "I AM."

It is with this understanding we have to read the Gospel of St. John. When we find the words: "I AM the Light of the world," we must interpret them quite literally. Now, what was this "I AM" which for the first time appeared in human form? It was the force of the Logos that united with the earth in the sunlight. Whenever the words "I" or "I AM" appear in St John's Gospel, realize that I AM was the name in which the initiates felt themselves united.

So Jesus was saying to his disciples: "That which is able to say "I AM" to itself, is the power of the Light of the World, and whoever follows after me will see in clear, waking consciousness." But the Pharisees, who clung to the old belief that the Light of Divine Love could only be planted within the human being at night, answered: "You call upon your "I AM" but we call upon Father Abraham. In this way we feel the power that justifies us to act as self-conscious beings. We feel ourselves strong and safe when we exist within the substance of the group soul that reaches back to Father Abraham." However Jesus replied: *"If one speaks of the I, as I speak, then the testimony is a true one; for I know that this I comes from the Father, from the very foundation of the world, and I know how it is to evolve in the future."* So John 8:15 should be understood as follows: "You judge all things according to the flesh, but I judge not the perishable that is in the flesh. And if I judge, then is my judgment true. For the I does not exist for itself alone, but it is united with the Father from whom it has descended." That is the meaning of this passage. If we understand the principle of the Father, we see that the words, *"Before Father Abraham was, was the I AM,"* contain the living essence of the Christian doctrine.

The purpose of our existence on this earth is to receive the full self-consciousness of the I AM. The fulfillment of our Christianity is, like Christ, to be one with God the Father as an I AM. So shall it be.

This is a rewrite of the end of Rudolf Steiner's Lecture 3 on The Gospel of St John.

♦

Four: The I AM gives Living Insight

"Again Jesus spoke to them, saying I AM the light of the world; he who follows me will not walk in darkness, but will have the light of life." John 8:12

In the last reflection we looked at the I AM as a new name for all those who unite with it. It is "so Old Testament" to give heredity prominence in our life. Those in whom the I AM is vibrant and alive should now call themselves David I AM, Kristina I AM, Julie I AM – together we belong to the I AM family. This is the picture of the future, of individuality and freedom.

John 8 speaks about the birth of the individual. It begins with the Pharisees bringing the woman caught in adultery. As they accuse her, Jesus had deep insight into their past lives and karma which he "wrote with his finger in the ground." Her accusers slithered away because through Jesus they also had insight into their own sins, their own karma.

What happens when we experience insight? What does it feel like at the moment of insight? Our being is lit up. We have the "light of life".

True insight allows the will to shoot up into our intelligence. Mostly our will slumbers in the depth of our being; this will is blind and our intelligence is abstract. We lazily regurgitate second hand information which contains nothing of our own self in it. Rev Mario Schoenmaker always said the only information worth having is firsthand information. "Every word I speak to you is second hand," he said. Steiner said, "You ought not to believe my words, but think them, that is to say, make them the object of your thinking."

To make spiritual truths the object of our thinking takes enormous strength of will. We have to strive to think through the thoughts, compare them with the thoughts that we already have and rigorously reach our own understanding. It is much easier to draw on other people's conclusions. If we resist this, when we have that personal insight we can feel the lightness of our will and the clarity of our mind. We feel alive. We have the "Ah ha" experience.

Blind will and abstract intelligence (second hand information regurgitated) are actually spiritual entities, spiritual beings who "walk in darkness", we know them as Ahriman and Lucifer.

Blind will and abstract intelligence do not live; only insight, which infuses our intelligence with will, is living. What does it mean to be alive, to be living? Anything that is alive is active; expanding and contracting (breathing) and metamorphosing (changing). To have the light of life is to have active insight. It means that the I AM is the captain of our soul; we are no longer a slave to second hand, lifeless information.

Furthermore, the I AM is our eternal essence, it is our personality; it is that part of us that endures from incarnation to incarnation. So through our "I" we have access to all our potentials. We are cut off from these potentials if we do not strive to connect with them, ie if we are lazy. The amount of effort we exert dictates the brightness of the I AM light that shines within our soul. If our I, our light, is not shining brightly in our soul then our astral is in charge, we walk in darkness and we are the tool of the anti-forces. Our insights are not original, our thoughts are abstract and our will is asleep.

If we allow the Light of the I AM to irradiate our soul, if we put effort into having personal insight, grappling with the truths spoken by Rev Mario Schoenmaker, Rudolf Steiner and others, then the thrilling words of John 8:32 will be a reality: "You will know the truth and the truth will set you free."

◆

3. I AM THE DOOR

One: Entering into Each Other

"I am the Door of the Sheep. All who came before me are thieves and robbers; but the sheep did not heed them." John 10:7

The first I AM - I Am the Bread of Life, directs our gaze downward, to the earth, to all that is beneath us which sustains our life. This includes all the minerals, the plants and animals.

The second I AM - I am the Light, directs our gaze upward. The light fills us from above. The light enables us to see and increasingly we can see all the dimensions of it, and eventually we will see spirit within matter.

The third I AM directs our gaze outward along the horizontal to that which lies before us - I am the Door. The fourth I AM directs our gaze within - I am the Good Shepherd. These four I AMs form a cross, the cross of our existence.

If our I AM is a door then we must ask: is it closed or shut? Most people in this world keep their door shut. They do not allow others in and nor do they go out to others. This is why there is so much anxiety and depression in the world, so much loneliness and sadness.

We don't have to preach Christ from a soap box, all we have to do is to show people how to open their doors, and how to enter through the doors of others. It is not just about opening our door or others opening their door, we have to dare to enter into others. It is a two-way thing.

How can we encourage people to open their door? If you see that someone is distressed about something, if you can get them to express just a little bit about their distress, you will have assisted them to open their door, maybe just a little bit, just enough for you to get your toe in. Although just a small opening, that still constitutes an open door. A gentle breeze of spirit can flow through a slightly open door.

When we are in distress preferring to keep things close to our chest then we experience the agony of bearing the weight alone. A lot of pressure and stale air can build up behind a closed door. If we are able to open our door, even if only slightly, then we will feel the relief of the gentle breeze of spirit on our face. Rev Mario Schoenmaker said several times that we could feel the presence of our spiritual companions as a gentle breeze blowing over us. This is what happened to the disciples after the crucifixion: "And when he had said this, he breathed on them, and said to them, "Receive the Holy Spirit." Jn 20:22

If we do find someone in distress and we do encourage them to open their door slightly, then we must take the opportunity to enter into them for it is only by putting ourselves 'in the other person's shoes' that we will be of any assistance to them. We must drop your own ideas and perspectives and enter into theirs. We can compare their position with ours but we cannot impose our position on them.

If we observe carefully - which is the constant cry, for esoteric teachings are not a complex and secret fandango, they are the result of careful observation and clear thinking - if we look closely we will see that people open their doors or keep them closed for the wrong reasons. Many people, even in our immediate vicinity, are tight-lipped about the things that should be openly discussed while at the same time they discuss openly things that are of little consequence. The door should be weighted according to spiritual principles.

Observation also reveals that people confuse earthly matters with spiritual matters. This does not raise earthly matters to spirit, it materializes spirit! Many of the so-called spiritual systems today are purely materialistic. It is not quite right to say that the sign of spiritual accomplishment is worldly success. That cannot be. Only spiritual success can come from spiritual work. If we achieve spiritual success then that will undoubtedly translate into earthly success because we are changed and our expression in the world is changed. What happens is that our doors will open a bit wider. And of course the key to this door is love. The greatest love is revealed to us in the Easter Deed. Easter is indeed a door.

◆

Two: Our Contribution to the Cosmos.

"I am the Door of the Sheep. All who came before me are thieves and robbers; but the sheep did not heed them." John 10:7

The I AM is a door to spirit. We are the sheep. On one side of the door are thieves and robbers snapping at our heels. On the other side of the door is our spiritualized being and our spiritual contribution to the Cosmos. These thieves and robbers are the forces within us that keep us from entering through the door. They keep us from entering into a right relationship with our I AM.

Have you ever walked into a room and had an uncomfortable feeling about happened there before you entered? You experience what another person has left behind in the room? The clairvoyant can see in an Imaginative picture what emanated from that person.

Do we think about what emanates from us every moment of everyday? In everything we do we send out spiritual substance into the world, it is perpetually passing over from us into the world. It rays forth from us and influences the whole world.

Every thought of love, every kindness, every prayer, and every lie, every judgment, all our irritability and our anger. These are actual substances, however fine, that ray forth and they are perceptible to those who have eyes to see. This substance continually fills the world and creates the future. This is how we provide the building-stones for the future. So it follows that the present world is the result of all the thoughts of love and hate from the past.

So we stand on the doorstep of the I AM in everyday life deciding to enter into that right relationship with it. Sometimes we can be objective and control our temper. Sometimes we can love where love is not returned. At other times we snap and abuse someone. Or we lie or cheat or blame others so that we don't have to take responsibility for what happens to us.

So what rays forth from us falls into two parts; that which is gladly received by the cosmos and that which the cosmos rejects. All that is negative does not please the cosmos so it leaves it alone. It remains where it is. How long does it remain? It remains there until such time as we come and destroy it. All false thoughts, all ugly feelings, whatever is morally evil - a man must himself erase from existence if it is to be no longer there. It will follow him continually until he has erased it. How is it erased? With true thoughts, beautiful feelings and good deeds.

Knowing this might motivate us to decide here and now never to create anything on the side of the door where the thieves and robbers are. But what about the 'stuff' that we have already created? Everyday we have the opportunity to deal with that. Yet how many people disown what they have created by not accepting responsibility for what is happening to them by blaming someone else?

If we want to pass through the door freely, having the right relationship to our I AM, then we must become the sheep, the sacrifice. If someone does us wrong then we must as quickly as possible neutralize our feelings about it. Otherwise those angry feelings will thieve and rob the forces of the I AM. We will create more substance that the Cosmos rejects.

This is exactly why the little tests of life come our way, to give us the opportunity to erase the past, nay, to redeem the past. Christ is the key to this process. He has given us the power that makes it possible to be continually creative, to continually create what the cosmos will accept. He stands there in the etheric world just on the other side of the door, patiently waiting for us – "I am the door, if any one enters by me, he will be saved, and will go in and out and find pasture."

It is awe inspiring to think that we can make this contribution to the cosmos. It is almost beyond comprehension that the light of our love, of our prayer, and the light that ignites when a spiritual truth thrills us, can create the future and resolve the past.

◆

Three: Prayer can Open the Door

"So Jesus again said to them, "Truly, truly, I say to you, I am the door of the sheep. All who came before me are thieves and robbers; but the sheep did not heed [hear] them. I am the door; if any one enters by me, he will be saved, and will go in and out and find pasture. The thief comes only to steal and kill and destroy; I came that they may have life, and have it abundantly." John 10:7-10

In the last reflection we considered the effect we can have on the cosmos. A right deed is accepted as a deposit in the cosmic bank account for all to use. The cosmos rejects our errors and leaves them there for us to put right one day.

Jesus says to us that the I AM is the door of the sheep. He points out that we can be the sheep who don't hear (or listen to) the thieves and robbers. Thieves and robbers are uninvited intruders, and intruders always operate out of self-interest. They enter to get something for themselves.

A door is an entrance, a point of passage from one place to another. One of the most important door openers in our life is prayer; when the door that connects this world to spiritual worlds is open which we go in and out of freely.

Many people don't use this door, or open it correctly, and some try to sneak through into the spiritual worlds without using the door. They intrude for self-gain. They think that they can acquire things that will advantage themselves. "Please God, take away this pain, take away this responsibility, this illness, help me to win the lottery, give me an easier life. Give me, give me, give me."

The riches, the abundant life, that comes from true prayer is beyond our earthly imagination. Prayer is a power. We can generate it at will and in full freedom. With our prayers we can assist others to open the door into the light. With our prayers we can surround a person with love so that they become aware of other ways to see things.

Rev Mario Schoenmaker spoke many wonderful prayers and spoke of ways to use prayer. He said that the future needed a totally new expression of prayer. He gave many examples of the power that prayer can have; how prayer is a door opener. He urged us to pray for the victims of the first gulf war in this way.

"Sit quietly and direct your thoughts and heart to the heavens. Picture in your mind people being killed and also see these souls floating in the universe. See their shock, their agony, and surround them with your light. Pray for their freedom, or use the special prayer I have written. After this be still for a little while, and then close with a good thought for yourself and all those whom you shall meet that day.

Let us fervently pray that this world will see the exalted Christ in all his glory and majesty." Rev Mario Schoenmaker 1991

That is a long, long way from the prayers that we have grown up with which always asked for something and demanded a response, "Please answer my prayer".

Our prayer will be different if it becomes a conversation with our best friend. The etheric Christ waits for us to consciously turn to him and speak as we would speak to a friend sitting beside us. For example, "Christ, my friend, Peter is not very strong at the moment; he is carrying the weight of world on his shoulders. I have tried to advise him to put down the load so that you can carry it for him, but he cannot. Christ, please take my prayer that he may be strengthened to carry the weight until he finds the wisdom to put it down."

If we see Christ as a real friend, if we work continually on our vision of Christ as our constant companion, then we will be able to speak to him as we do to our friends. We don't ask our friends to give us this and that all the time do we? We have been brought up not to ask others to give us things. I remember when I was quite small my mother would say, "Don't ask people for things, wait until they offer you something." ... hopefully lollies (candy) I thought at the time. I also remember thinking: how will they know what I want?

Christ knows what we want, or rather, what we need. Our prayer can strengthen others as it can strengthen us to take life in our stride. Then our prayer opens the door and we can go in and out and find pasture, and have life abundantly so that we become life-givers. Rev Mario Schoenmaker says:

"It is our calling to pray to God on behalf of other souls who cannot do it for themselves. To intercede for them is a priestly function … whether you are ordained or not. In that sense all our prayers are as strong and as fertile as the prayers of those who may be priests. Our prayer can give a spiritual power to the world, to the cosmos and to the hierarchy. As such all of us are part of this great cosmic movement which we call the Christ."

♦

Four: Clairvoyance through Rigorous Thinking

So Jesus again said to them, "Truly, truly, I say to you, I am the door of the sheep. All who came before me are thieves and robbers; but the sheep did not heed them. I am the door; if any one enters by me, he will be saved, and will go in and out and find pasture. The thief comes only to steal and kill and destroy; I came that they may have life, and have it abundantly. John 10:7-10

The preceding verses are about Jesus who has healed a man born blind.

Jesus said, "For judgment I came into this world, that those who do not see may see, and that those who see may become blind." Some of the Pharisees near him heard this, and they said to him, "Are we also blind?" Jesus said to them, "If you were blind, you would have no guilt; but now that you say, 'We see,' your guilt remains. John 9:39-41

This reminds us of Genesis and the fall doesn't it? – the guilty pair saw that they were naked.

There is a great problem in this world with guilt, sin and karma. Fortunately many people are blind to the things that they do. If they could see the consequences of their actions they could get quite a shock.

Then there are others who say that Christ has taken care of karma – he may have cancelled karma but does he do it continually? Does he continually cancel all the new karma we create? We have just been considering this haven't we? The cosmos rejects our errors and leaves them there for us to put right one day. The whole thing hinges on seeing.

Jesus said: I am the Door. Seeing is a door isn't it? Seeing into the spiritual worlds means we pass through the door to spirit. The man born blind is us when we are not clairvoyant, not clear-seeing. But if we see ... our guilt remains. So Christ doesn't cancel karma when we have our clear spiritual sight and we sin.

Many of us aspire to this ability to see clearly, to see what it really going on. There are three types of people in this world. Those who have retained the old instinctive clairvoyance, they speak with spirits and they say they are channeling or talking to dead grandma. Then there are those who have lost that clairvoyance, they move around the world totally dependent on the earthly brain. Then there are those with a budding new clairvoyance, those who are using their pure thinking.

In terms of human evolution we are in an intermediate stage because we must experience a feeling of inner freedom. This means that we become blind, lose our old clairvoyance, and then through our I AM develop our spiritual eyes. This is the sight that enables us to see into the world that we will enter when we die, our spiritual homeland. But we have to develop this sight here on earth. Our physical eye was developed in our pre-earthly life, before we were born; so the spiritual eye must be acquired here on earth, before we die.

How is this eye developed? Through thinking. Through active spiritual knowledge. With healthy intelligence we can think deeply about a thing and have a spiritual understanding of it. If only we are prepared to think the thing out, and then feel it through and through. It is not clairvoyance but the activity of wrestling with knowledge that gives us spiritual eyes to use here and to use after death.

If we do have a clairvoyant insight we must work with it to bring it down into our earthly mind, into our thinking. A spiritual insight will vanish after a few days unless we grasp it and make worldly sense of it. We have to actively grasp the fleeting thoughts and bring them to the level of ordinary understanding. If we are given a clairvoyant insight by another person then to truly receive it we need to understand it in the very same way in which it is understood by them when they communicated it – otherwise, of what use is it?

So clairvoyance is not the essential task of man on earth. The task of man on earth is to understand the supersensible truths with ordinary, healthy human understanding. This is the pasture. That is exactly why Jesus says "I Am the door."

♦

Five: Entering into Others

So Jesus again said to them, "Truly, truly, I say to you, I am the door of the sheep. All who came before me are thieves and robbers; but the sheep did not heed them. I am the door; if any one enters by me, he will be saved, and will go in and out and find pasture. The thief comes only to steal and kill and destroy; I came that they may have life, and have it abundantly. John 10:7-10

In the last reflection we considered the new clairvoyance – insight through rigorous thinking. We saw how this insight brings with it a spiritual responsibility. We live in a time when we are hardly conscious of the workings of our soul and our I AM, we struggle to escape the idea that we are a physical body moving around in the world.

Just for a moment picture yourself as an "I" walking down the street and you meet a friend and they also have an "I". Remember that your soul and your "I" are like a cloud around you. This cloud penetrates your body and it also mingles with all that is outside your skin. Think of the Roadrunner in slow motion.

When our "I" encounters another "I", in order to grasp the other "I" we have to penetrate into the nature of the other person. Or it may even be a tree or an animal. So if you and I meet your "I" has to enter into me. This might appear to be a simple and straightforward thing. Wouldn't your "I" and my "I" have to be compatible for you to enter into me and vice versa? Wouldn't this explain why we are uncomfortable with some people; we are not able to enter into them or they won't let us enter into them?

Now if our "I" is going to enter into someone it must become like a sheep; a simple, innocent being who has surrendered. What would our "I" surrender? All its understanding and knowledge! For a moment we must become an ego-less being.

If we want to enter into the other person we have to strip ourselves off, leave everything outside; it's the story of initiation, of going into the temple. We cannot fully enter into another person with all our own preconceived ideas. Not only that, we also have to know ourselves. We have to be able differentiate ourselves from the other person when we enter into them.

So when we are inside the other person our "I" takes a

snapshot of the other person, a copy of what is going on in the other person during our exchange. Then we withdraw back into ourselves to see if the copy of their inner being (to the extent that we could enter into it) is compatible with our inner being. Does the copy please us or not? Can we understand it or not, is it similar to some of the things we have in ourselves or is it too different?

If the Christ Impulse is active within us, and our I AM has a strong connection with our inner being, then we will be able to be very objective. It is our "I" that is constantly trying to bring itself into harmony, in-tune with, the copy of the other person. If what we find warms us we form a bond, we easily connect with the other person.

This reveals how disagreements arise - these are the thieves and robbers. We can't go in and out and find pasture if our lower untamed soul levels rise up in a murky fog of like and dislike. If we are too busy with self we can't take the other person in. How easy it is for us to kill and destroy others with our misunderstanding thoughts. We kill and destroy our relationships. All because we want to take a stand and we can't enter into the other person or let them enter into us.

Sure, it may not always be wise to enter into another person, but we must continually strive for the higher I AM state of being. Those of us who were taught by Rev Mario Schoenmaker (or no doubt any other spiritual teacher) had the experience of being deeply known by him. We allowed him to enter into us, we trusted him, and in that trust he could teach us. Since his death some people even say that they feel they will never be known like that again. Rev Mario had such control of his "I" that he could enter into you, experience you totally and come back into himself and give you the advice you knew you needed to hear. Let us always strive to be the sheep led by the Good Shepherd so that we can move in and out of each other freely and find pasture.

♦

4. I AM THE GOOD SHEPHERD

One: The I AM and the Hireling

I am the good shepherd. The good shepherd lays down his life for the sheep. He who is a hireling and not a shepherd, whose own the sheep are not, sees the wolf coming and leaves the sheep and flees; and the wolf snatches them and scatters them. He flees because he is a hireling and cares nothing for the sheep. I am the good shepherd; I know my own and my own know me, as the Father knows me and I know the Father; and I lay down my life for the sheep. And I have other sheep, that are not of this fold; I must bring them also, and they will heed my voice. So there shall be one flock, one shepherd. For this reason the Father loves me, because I lay down my life, that I may take it again. No one takes it from me, but I lay it down of my own accord. I have power to lay it down, and I have power to take it again; this charge I have received from my Father. John 10:11-18

It is hard to imagine the life of a shepherd today. For this story to speak to us we must try to experience the relationship between sheep and shepherd; the sense of security that comes from the shepherd and the innocence of the sheep. There is obviously something special about the sheep because they need to be tended by a human both night and day. It is a picture of goodness and purity isn't it?

Jesus tells us that our I AM is this good shepherd, it stands like a sentinel, guiding and guarding the sheep. Another question arises:

41

what is a shepherd without sheep? There is deep importance attached to both sides; the sheep need a shepherd and the shepherd needs the sheep.

So the living Imagination that comes from this pastoral scene is that the shepherd is our I AM, our Real Self which lives in the heavens. The sheep are all the faculties and forces within us that are budding and growing. The hireling is our little "I", the worldly sense-of-self that is merely a reflection of our Real Self. Because the I AM can't gain access to us until our faculties and forces are mature enough it has to call in a contractor.

Just look at this hireling. I don't know who hired it; they clearly didn't look at the job description. It's got no experience; it doesn't have any sheep of its own. It is a coward, afraid of wolves, it won't lay down its life for the sheep and it doesn't know its own.

If we want to know about the I AM we can reverse these things. The I AM is full of courage and boldness, it is not afraid of the wolves - the devouring forces in and around us. It will lay down its life; it willingly enters into this earth sphere. And it knows its own; there is a recognition beyond fear or favor. These are the marks of an I AM that is engaged as fully as possible in the earthly life of our being.

Our I AM is the shepherd who can keep the wolves away from the tender levels of your soul and spirit. We need this shepherd at this crucial time in the evolution of mankind. We are developing our consciousness soul level which is the catalyst for the budding of the Spirit Self which in turn causes the Life Spirit to stir. Also, at the same time we have to integrate our I AM more fully. Yet the astral thinks that because it has been around for so long it is up to the task. It tries to convince the small "I" to listen to it rather than to the great I AM.

If we do not continually and consciously use our Imagination to create a relationship with our I AM, our Real Self, our small "I" will scatter our forces and we will be vulnerable to attacks.

Our small "I" cares nothing for the sheep, those small budding forces of consciousness. The astral, which always seeks out the comfort zones, says in a loud voice: "It takes so much effort to develop consciousness, take a rest, have a snooze, have this psychic vision instead. Live in the levels of like and dislike, half-baked ideas and cliquey groups."

The I AM sees Christ in us and Christ in every person. "I know my own and my own know me" The tentative connection we have with our I AM at this point in time means that we must continually remind ourselves of this. There is a oneness, a unity, and we are part of it. Yet when we look around the world, like Alcibiades, speaking of an aged Socrates, we may say, "A poor dwelling, but in it lives a God."

We must try to be more and more conscious of the I AM that wants to shepherd the tender and innocent consciousness in us, and to keep it from the wolves. So whenever we feel scattered we can be sure that our small "I" has listened to our astral which has fled in the face of opposition.

♦

Two: Karma, the Opportunity

The thief comes only to steal and kill and destroy; I came that they may have life, and have it abundantly. I am the good shepherd. The good shepherd lays down his life for the sheep. He who is a hireling and not a shepherd, whose own the sheep are not, sees the wolf coming and leaves the sheep and flees; and the wolf snatches them and scatters them. He flees because he is a hireling and cares nothing for the sheep. I am the good shepherd; I know my own and my own know me, as the Father knows me and I know the Father; and I lay down my life for the sheep. John 10:11 - 15

Last time we reflected on the Real I and its mirrored reflection, the small I, the hireling, which doesn't always do a good job. One of the areas in our life where the small I leads us astray is when we have to deal with our karma.

We know that every night when we go to sleep our small I leaves our body lying in the bed and it goes into the heavens and has many experiences. Wouldn't it be fantastic if we could be conscious of where it goes and what it does? ... Or would it?

Do you know what it does? it has a heart to heart chat with the Real I who reminds it of the purpose of incarnation and the karma that must be faced. And what is the purpose of incarnation? To grow in consciousness, to become more aware of reality ... so then we *can* know what the small I is doing at night when it roams the universe. I remember Rev Mario Schoenmaker telling us in his Sunday afternoon discourses on St Mark in the 1980s - we would all squash into an upstairs room at Palm Court Manor - about how our I and our astral left us at night and then one day he said, but often they don't even leave your room! It all depends on the state of our consciousness.

There are ways to ensure that we leave our bedroom at night when our body sleeps. One of them is to occupy ourselves with ideals during the day instead of thinking and speaking about trivia. This connects us up with the Archangels. Another way is to have a sincere interest in others through a true and genuine love. Not just an interest in those we like, and ignoring those we don't like. This connects us up with the Archai at night.

So at night if we have the right connection with the Hierarchy we get in touch with our destiny, our karma. We awake in the morning strengthened to face the obstacles, the wolves, which always try to scatter and snatch our budding consciousness.

So the love or the hatred (the two extremes in our soul) we express during the day is the creative force of karma that weaves our destiny. It is wrong to say 'I am ill or I have experienced misfortune – it is my karma!' Karma is not a fixed thing; it is always coming into being. Our dis-ease may not be due to the past; it may simply be an opportunity for our consciousness to grow. Karma is not a punishment. It weaves into our life to assist us to move forward. To experience the truth of this we also need a deep sense of the justice that rules and balances this world.

Ask yourself: Do I want my consciousness to grow? At the same time ask yourself: Do I want life to be sweet and lovely all the time? If we were only ever to experience what we wish for ourselves we would be weaklings.

An uneventful life produces weakness of soul, the weaker our soul the less the Shepherd can tend our budding consciousness, and the more the hireling has to do the job. So we must strive to give our thoughts and words the wings of idealism rather than the weight of trivia. We must strive to place ourselves in the other person's shoes more often. Then, when misfortune comes our way we realize that it is a gift, we stand our ground, and can't be scattered and the forces that stir within us will sustain us. These are the forces that come from the Shepherd. Stare that old wolf in the eyes and say: I know your tricks, you want me to seek comfort, and you don't want me to have a consciousness of my Real Self.

In these moments we can try to visualize the Shepherd standing there, willing to lay down his life that we may have the new consciousness, the third consciousness, the mind of Christ.

It is wonderful to think that the effort we make in our daily life strengthens our consciousness. Just think of the benefits when we sleep, and after death when we are born into spirit. To the degree we are conscious here is the degree that we will be conscious there. Conscious of the Angels, Archangels and Archai, and how, in turn, we assist them to do their work. Then, in turn, reveal to us of the opportunities we have to expand our consciousness while in our bodies in this world. It fills us with gratitude that we can know something of these truths, the truth that sets us free.

Ideas from "The Forming of Destiny in Sleeping and Waking"
by Rudolf Steiner 6.4.1923

♦

Three: Other Sheep – Other Opinions, Other Streams

I am the good shepherd. The good shepherd lays down his life for the sheep. He who is a hireling and not a shepherd, whose own the sheep are not, sees the wolf coming and leaves the sheep and flees; and the wolf snatches them and scatters them. He flees because he is a hireling and cares nothing for the sheep. I am the good shepherd; I know my own and my own know me, as the Father knows me and I know the Father; and I lay down my life for the sheep. And I have other sheep, that are not of this fold; I must bring them also, and they will heed my voice. So there shall be one flock, one shepherd. For this reason the Father loves me, because I lay down my life, that I may take it again. No one takes it from me, but I lay it down of my own accord. I have power to lay it down, and I have power to take it again; this charge I have received from my Father." John 10:11 -18

Verse 17 seems to be at odds with this fourth I AM saying; we can accept that the wolves have their place, but what about "other sheep"?

And I have other sheep, that are not of this fold; I must bring them also, and they will heed my voice. So there shall be one flock, one shepherd. Verse 17

We can look at this in two ways; an inner way and an outer way. We have been looking at the sheep as parts of our growing consciousness. One thing about our consciousness is that it is full of ideas and opinions. And we love to be right don't we? If we are really honest, we often prefer it if others are wrong and we are right.

Yet to reach a full understanding of something we need many different points of view. The opinions of others contribute to the whole. Think about a large tree, each person's view of it will differ. Some say, "Oh let's have a holistic view, let's look from a distance so we can see the whole thing - one elevated, holistic but blurry view. One person can never see every side of a tree at once. We can only really get a full picture of the tree when we take into account all the perspectives.

The secret lies in accepting the other person's view that differs from our own. If we cannot immediately see it then we should hold their view in our heart until we can see how it gives our view another dimension or, if not, that we discard it. How often do we discard or dismiss another's viewpoint too soon? To honor the view of others when it differs from our own requires effort. This striving for truth, the effort we put in, is like giving our soul a work-out.

Another way to look at these "other sheep" is to look outside ourselves. In the previous reflection we considered karma not as punishment but as something that provides the necessary resistance to propel us forward. Just like an airplane cannot soar into the air until it meets with the required resistance.

This resistance can come from people steeped in different belief systems. Or it can come from people within our own belief system who have come up through a different stream of the mystery teachings. When we reach the point of remembering our past lives we will see all the different streams that we have dedicated ourselves to life after life. There were healers – in Atlantis, Egypt, Palestine etc., there were astrologers, there were musicians, temple dancers, there were teachers of the mysteries, oracles, knights, builders, hunters, scientists, the list goes on - each skill appropriate for its time.

Many of these skills can no longer be used for consciousness has changed. Yet each one of us has a certain number of skills in our soul memory, some of which can be used now but in a different way. As memory awakens in people everywhere, as it is at present – even unconsciously- we can see that many people want to drag these old gifts into the present. But our I AM is not interested in that; the I AM is a unifier – there will be one flock and one shepherd. What works against this unification is like and dislike; sympathy and antipathy. The old memories, of different tribes, different cultures, different belief systems, rise up and we are at odds with each other face to face or behind the other person's back we gossip. It's best not to be too self-righteous and place this in the other person's arena.

This is simply the karma of the different streams. "I have other sheep that are not of this fold." There are many theories about 2 streams, 3 streams and 4 streams but there could possibly be 12 streams and they may be linked to the zodiac. The issue is not how many streams but the unification that is necessary now.

Because we live in the presence of the etheric Christ these other sheep are hearing the voice of the Shepherd. We are coming together in groups to unify. Great teachers are unifiers and when they die the atmosphere of the different streams gives rise to factionalism. Now it is up to each person to act in a unified way. Karma is the opportunity to unify. Perhaps we could spell 'karma' a bit differently – c a l m e r.

By finding ways to embrace differences we will work with the Good Shepherd and hear his voice. The best way to get over any dislike we may have is to love. We don't have to like a person to love them. It is our challenge today; to transform our likes and dislikes into love.

To stay calm in our differences, to embrace all points of view to see the whole, and to love where love may not be returned ensures that we will not become estranged from the I AM.

◆

Four: Shepherds and Gods

I am the good shepherd. The good shepherd lays down his life for the sheep. .... I am the good shepherd; I know my own and my own know me John 10:11 & 14

Shepherds appear at important places in the bible. And sometimes angels appear to shepherds. Two very important places that this happens is:

One - the announcement of the birth of Christ in Luke 2:8. The angels announce to the Shepherd that the great I AM is about to incarnate.

Two - in Exodus 3 when we first hear about this I AM.

"Now Moses was keeping the flock of his father-in-law, ... And the angel of the LORD appeared to him in a flame of fire out of the midst of a bush; and he looked, and lo, the bush was burning, yet it was not consumed. And Moses said, "I will turn aside and see this great sight, why the bush is not burnt." When the LORD saw that he turned aside to see, God called to him out of the bush, "Moses, Moses!" And he said, "Here am I." Ex 3:1ff

God then gave Moses quite a bit of advice about bringing the people out of Egypt, out of the darkness and it continues:

... Then Moses said to God, "If I come to the people of Israel and say to them, 'The God of your fathers has sent me to you,' and they ask me, 'What is his name?' what shall I say to them?" God said to Moses, "I AM who I AM." And he said, "Say this to the people of Israel, 'I AM has sent me to you.'"

Without being a Hebrew scholar it doesn't take much to imagine that word 'who' - I am 'who' I am - was placed there to satisfy the material mind.

Surely this God really said I AM the I AM. Therefore if we are striving to become the I AM doesn't that mean that we are striving to become a God? It really is an awesome consideration.

Look around the world; people are bleeding rivers of blood in the name of peace. People are hateful, angry, hurting, and resentful. They cry for compensation for their misfortunes. Why can't they see that they are becoming Gods? that their misfortune is the path to becoming a God!

It's agony this business of becoming a God, this moving out of the darkness of our unconsciousness. It is an entirely different view if we see the Gods-in-the-making all around us each day.

Is it possible to say that we love Christ and then hate the other person, that God-in-the-making? Wouldn't that mean that we crucify Christ again and again? In Matthew we read those powerful words, *"whatever you do to least of these, you do to me?"*

That is what the I AM is all about. The more connected we are with our I AM the more fully we feel the other person's sorrow, pain and joy as if it was our own. The less self-absorbed we are, and the more we can see things from the other person's point of view.

The more integrated our I AM is the less we criticize or judge because we know how that degrades the other person. If they are degraded then so are we. We don't put ourselves down either; we must strive to honestly assess ourselves. Not to overrate or underrate. Then we see, patiently, that we are all moving forward in our own way. We can never think that we greater or more advanced; just taking a different route. Who knows whose route is longer or shorter? Hebrews 13 tells us that *"Some have entertained angels unawares."*

It is interesting that fear, anxiety, hatred and anger seem to be increasing. This is actually a good sign because it is proof of the proximity of the I AM. The I AM exerts pressure on us as it tries to connect with us. The great Shepherd is calling, his voice is urgent. It is up to us to hear his voice saying, 'Raise your consciousness. See the possibilities of the I AM, you are gods-in-the-making. Don't shrink back from the discomfort, don't try to escape or withdraw, never mind about feeling insecure. Embrace these things knowing that within them you will find your I AM.'

♦

Five: Don't Cling to Karma

For this reason the Father loves me, because I lay down my life, that I may take it again. No one takes it from me, but I lay it down of my own accord. I have power to lay it down, and I have power to take it again; this charge I have received from my Father." John 10:17-18

These words speak about the ultimate sacrifice. To sacrifice our life ... and the prerequisite is that we actually have something to sacrifice. This sacrifice is not that of a soldier fighting for his country, or a quasi-martyr suicide bomber. This is the shepherd giving his life for his sheep. This is about the gentle and good shepherd and the pure and innocent sheep.

The evolution of our consciousness is at a crucial point. It must become clear-seeing, insightful. We must attain to a consciousness that has the power to lay down life, and the power to take it up again. This is about self-control isn't it?

What is this life? It is the life force in us, it is our soul-filled etheric - *psuche* in the Greek. When we have this life force we are alive, when it leaves us we are dead. This life force, the etheric, is the domain of thinking and memory. Our etheric body is also the home of temperament, character, inclinations; all of which are molded by our experiences in past lives. So in our etheric are our memories of the past; from this life and previous lives.

How often are we willing to lay down our thoughts, our memories, our temperament? Can we lay down our memories from past lives? A thorough examination in this area will reveal that we love our thoughts, we love our memories and we persist in our temperament no matter the pain.

In the third reflection of the previous I AM saying "I Am the Door of Sheep" - which is closely linked to this I AM saying - we spoke about karma. Our good deeds are accepted as a deposit in the cosmic bank account for everyone to use. When we do the wrong thing the cosmos rejects these errors and leaves them there for us to put right one day.

This speaks of self-redemption; that we must work out our karma alone. It seems to contradict the Christian message that Christ died for our sins. The truth about karma is not that we should just try to live peacefully because Christ has taken care of our sins, or that we should slog it out till the end of time redeeming all our dastardly deeds. The truth lies in the middle.

The one who is stronger can always lend a hand to the one who struggles under the weight of karma. The Christ deed exemplifies this. The strongest of all came to lift the weight of karma. The more we take the Christ force into ourselves the lighter our weight, and more able we are to lighten the load for the other person (but only at their invitation of course).

We do not have to act out of our unconscious life-force which is the ledger of all rights and wrongs. We can lay down this life ... Jesus says: *"I lay down my life, that I may take it again. No one takes it from me, but I lay it down of my own accord. I have power to lay it down, and I have power to take it again;"*

It is the I AM that gives us the power and the strength to do this. The more we engage with our I AM and the more we place Christ in the midst of us the easier it will be to lay down the memories, the thoughts, the temperament that incites us to retaliate at times. Although, we are not going to succeed every time; some karma just bites us on the backside.

But as we grow in consciousness we will remember to turn to the Shepherd. By becoming more and more aware that within us is this Shepherd, this guide, the knower of our Real Self, always watchful, always encouraging us to do the good and to neutralize the bad deeds of the past. The shepherd is always there; we just have to hear his voice. His voice is sometimes drowned out by fear; fear that the Shepherd will urge us to do something we would rather not do. It is the Christ impulse that gives us a love that knows no fear; a love that makes us whole and free.

◆

5. I AM THE RESURRECTION AND THE LIFE

One: The I AM Imagination

We have reached the very depths of the Gospel of St John now. This is the chapter about the raising of Lazarus. Lazarus is ill, Jesus says its ok but then Lazarus dies and Mary and Martha accuse Jesus of neglecting what they see as his duty. The fifth I Am saying erupts from the middle of the story.

Jesus said to her, "I am the resurrection and the life; he who believes in me, though he die, yet shall he live, and whoever lives and believes in me shall never die. Do you believe this?" John 11:25f

The raising of Lazarus heralds the real power of the I AM. This is the power that is to be at the disposal of every individual person - a resurrection power. So two thousand years ago we were given personal access to our I AM and today we hardly know what this I AM is. Consequently this resurrection power remains a mystery.

If we contemplate the activities of Christ as they are reported in sacred writings we will begin to experience its characteristics. Christ is the key that gives us unrestricted access to our I AM which dwells mainly outside our being. This access is a two-way process; our action and its response. In our reaching out we signal our willingness to receive its activity into our being. As we develop trust we allow the I AM more and more access to our daily lives; it in turn works more fully in us.

A great tool for building an understanding of our I AM and its power is Imagination. Through active Imagination we can create a reality for ourselves about our relationship with our I AM. The following framework is one way that we can develop our own personal I AM Imagination.

Imagine your being as an egg-shaped, multi-colored mist extending outside, around and through your physical body. At the center of this mist is a tiny spark – your self, the part you are speaking from when you say "I". Your I AM, your Real Self, is outside this egg. See this Real Self as a golden mist, reaching down to your multi-colored being. Sometimes it touches the surface of your being, sometimes it withdraws into the universe. See it as a flowing, continual movement like gentle waves kissing the shore. Sometimes the sun, the light of Christ, glistens in this golden mist making it finer and lighter, dancing. Sometimes the sunlit mist shines into your egg-shaped being like light through a dark forest. It is as if a pathway opened up in your being and your Real Self could engage with your small "I", the tiny spark. This would happen at times when we are less anxious, more peaceful, more giving and thoughtful. Imagine the tiny spark starting to flicker into a small flame within you. See it flickering up to the golden mist that is your Real Self. Become aware that you feel light and strong and calm when this connection is made.

As you maintain this connection direct your attention to your posture. Experience the uprightness of your physical body; feel as tall and straight as the letter "I". ... Now move your attention to your voice. Think about the power of your voice, the tone of your voice, the sound it makes as it forms words. ... Then direct your attention to your thoughts. Remember how you feel when your thoughts are clear and concise. The satisfaction when you are able to work through to a solution. This is when you are really conscious.

This is the resurrection power within our being. We have raised our consciousness out of the tomb of our body. We have become conscious of the fullness of our being. Remember this feeling. We can bring this resurrection experience to mind often during the day.

Another resurrection experience is to imagine being with the disciples when they encountered the resurrected Christ. In your imagination see Christ standing before you saying, "Peace be with you" - keep doing it till you feel the reality of it. You will feel a peace actually flow through you, raising you up. Your whole being will feel lighter, finer. If we practice it often enough then we are able to use it during the day whenever we need it. When we experience fear, annoyance, judgment from another person, or find ourselves quick to judge others we can interrupt the thoughts and feelings with the "Peace be with you."

John records the story of the disciples seeing the risen Christ in chapter 20 - imagine their fear! Have you ever seen a ghost? Seeing one in the movies is frightening enough. Or imagine that a spiritual being has manifested beside you in the room. Then as quickly as you can let those words "Peace be with you" wash over you and feel the fear subside.

These resurrection exercises are not techniques; they are a way of life. They are as essential as breathing or eating and drinking. If we are to have Life we must connect up with our I AM. We must have regular doses of I AM in our daily activities. If we don't we will die and there will be no resurrection.

Christ left us the ritual of bread and wine to remind us of the resurrection power. He is the great I AM that enters the flesh, transmutes the blood and promises that if we believe in the I AM, though we are dead, yet shall we live, and whoever lives and believes in the I AM shall never die. Do you believe this?

◆

Two: Death & Resurrection of a Christened Person

Soul Mass for Michael Stonehouse

Read John 11:1-27 The fifth I Am saying is this: *Jesus said to her, "I am the resurrection and the life; he who believes in me [I AM], though he die, yet shall he live, and whoever lives and believes in me [I AM] shall never die. Do you believe this?" John 11:25f*

The journey of life is all about separation, initiation, and renewal. Renewal is of course a raising up, a resurrection.

Our birth is a separation, our life is an initiation and our death is a renewal, a resurrection.

Jesus uses his response to Martha to speak to us about the resurrection power that is available to us through our I AM. The two examples of this are the two different types of death in the gospel of St John; the death and revival of Lazarus and the death and resurrection of Christ. One revives the physical body and one resurrects to a spiritual body. Both speak of initiation.

How interesting that we should be at this point in our reflections on the I AM sayings as we celebrate the passing of our friend Michael who was born into spirit a few days ago (5.7.2003).

We can assist Michael's soul to awaken in the spiritual worlds. It is through his I AM that Michael will become conscious – "he who believes in me (I AM), though he die, yet shall he live". We are dedicating all the love and light we can generate in this gathering to him. We pray that he awakens and becomes as conscious as possible, as soon as possible.

We can use our imagination to be conscious of Michael's being expanding into the region between the earth and the moon as he begins the journey of his new life. Because he so loved The Centre, and Rev Mario Schoenmaker and his teachings, Michael will long for the sustenance he experienced with us. We can be of great assistance to him. When we read the teachings Michael will draw near to learn. He will be able to learn more now that he is free of his physical brain. He in turn can give us new understandings because he now participates in the spiritual worlds where truth is unfettered by physical constraints. We should also bring him to mind in our prayer.

Michael has now shed his physical vehicle and so he lives in his etheric body. Its forces, no longer required to maintain the physical body, are now dedicated to the review of his earthly life. This is what Michael has been doing over the last few days.

If all things go according to the cosmic plan, today his etheric will start to separate from his astral. Part of it he will take with him as he journey's further, part of it he will leave behind in the earth's atmosphere. Because Michael has been so devoted to Christ for so many years his etheric is a living force.

Over the next few days Michael will be giving a great gift to this earth. His Christed etheric forces with be deposited in the etheric sphere of this earth and will enliven it. We give thanks to Michael for this gift. It is an important gift because so many people ignore the etheric presence of Christ and this causes the etheric sphere around this world to harden.

Indeed, every soul that becomes aware of the etheric presence of Christ during his life leaves such a great gift for this world when they die. This is the resurrection power of the I AM at work.

Over the next few months thoughts of Michael may come to you, at these moments think of him with love and with gratitude for all that he gave, his devotion, his quiet giving attitude. These are the things that help his soul dwell in the spiritual light and keep the darkness away.

When someone we know and love finishes their earthly life it is good to contemplate that the absence of a physical body does not mean that the soul is absent. *"I am the resurrection and the life; he who believes in me, though he die, yet shall he live"* - The I AM is eternal, the Christed I AM is indestructible – and whoever lives and believes in me- the I AM - shall never die. And then Jesus says, *"Do you believe this?"* can you feel him saying it directly to you. *"Do you believe this?"* For believing it has great power.

Jesus spoke these words just before he demonstrated the power of the I AM to revive, to resurrect, to raise up life. Michael has now been raised up. We can assist him on his journey to a higher, resurrected life so that when he returns to this earth again he will be a greater co-worker with Christ. "Do you believe this?"

♦

Three: Conscience; Raising Astral to I AM

Jesus said to her, "I am the resurrection and the life; he who believes in me, though he die, yet shall he live, and whoever lives and believes in me shall never die. Do you believe this?" John 11:25f

This world does not want us to believe in the I AM, the lord of this world, Ahriman, knows that the I AM is imminent. He is very busy calculating the ways to rob us of our I AM opportunities.

Take conscience as an example. Many people seem to have no conscience; they decide to do whatever they like and think that they will get away with it. Two thousand years ago the word 'conscience' appeared in our language for the first time. Before that we didn't need a conscience; if our deeds were bad the Furies tormented us. So if we told a lie, or stole something, a spooky Furie would attach itself to us so that we - and everybody else - knew that we had made the wrong decision.

As human consciousness developed the word conscience began appearing in ancient Greek literature. This indicated that conscience was internalized and this event coincided with the earthly presence of the I AM. The departure of the Furies signaled the development of external laws; our legal system today stands on this development.

The interesting thing, however, is that the I AM is self-regulating. A person who has a strong connection to their I AM does not need to be regulated by laws so that they do the right thing. So why is it that almost every day a new law is announced? No doubt the lord of this world is at work because these laws supplant the inherent ability of the I AM to do the good?

Whenever freedom is curtailed people do not believe in the I AM. Whenever there is no trust, where there is doubt, people do not believe in the I AM. Jesus is speaking this fifth I AM saying to Martha who didn't trust the I AM. The feminine within us, the soul levels, are drawn towards the astral when the I AM draws close. It is the astral that must be raised up by the I AM. The astral must become spiritualized, it must leave its instinctual, psychic ways and become conscious and clear seeing (clair-voyant).

Jesus says (the) I AM is the resurrection and the life ... but only if we believe it!

The resurrection body of Christ exists. It is a reality. It is a constant presence in and around us. If we can't see it we just have to believe it. Each year between Easter and Pentecost the resurrection is replayed so that we can re-experience the intensity of it. If we believe it then each year our experience of it will be more intense.

Those who do not experience this resurrection power experience instead a schism between their I AM and their physical existence. The evidence of this can be observed in the daily news: an increase in violence, the degradation of sex and the abuse of substances. The dignity and divinity of the human being is lowered or lost.

Rev. Mario Schoenmaker continually spoke of the resurrection power. He said, "I want to use the words 'chemical marriage' to indicate the gradual absorption of the resurrection forces of Christ into the human organism. So a harmony which we once lost through the fall will now be restored and re-established within us."

In another place Rev Mario spoke of his anxiety about the teachings being used in a clever and theoretical way. "If we cannot unite that sense of responsibility, if we cannot unite the fullness of our emotional or our feeling forces in order to break this [theoretical] tendency then we cannot participate of that resurrection power that is available in the world today."

Then in response to the most frequently asked question – what is my purpose - he said, "the purpose of us being together as a group is precisely that as a group we develop such a love for the spiritual worlds, such a love for Christ that one day he will be here and you will see him. That becomes for you the second resurrection as the Book of Revelation says."

The sign of the resurrection power is the bread and the wine. When Jesus, at the last supper, blessed the bread and the wine, he gave thanks for the hidden forces that create them; the fermentation of the grape and yeast. The fermentation is the resurrection power at work in the wheat and the grape.

If we participate in the consecration and eat the bread and the wine it is not to be 'religious' but to experience the resurrection power through which we can see the living Christ. Christ no longer nailed to the cross of this world but risen to be our constant companion in everything we do till the end of this world. Then we do not need laws, our conscience will guide us.

♦

Four: Becoming more Conscious

Jesus said to her, "I am the resurrection and the life; he who believes in me, though he die, yet shall he live, and whoever lives and believes in me shall never die. Do you believe this?" John 11:25f

To be dead means to be unconscious. So "whoever lives" is conscious and can see into the spiritual worlds as clearly as they see into the physical world.

Although most of us have some more work to do in this area, it is not an impossible task; we can make a beginning and there are many aids. Knowledge, real spiritual truth is the best aid. Not theory, as we spoke of it in the last reflection, but living knowledge that quickens us.

Connecting with our I AM resurrects our consciousness from a dead earthly consciousness to a living spiritual consciousness. This does not mean to be psychic; when we are psychic our consciousness is lowered. Anything that lowers or removes consciousness belongs to the past, it is not part of our current evolution and the I AM will have nothing to do with it. Clairvoyance is about thinking, pure thinking, a resurrected living thinking that gives insight into the reality of the cosmos.

Many people are becoming and more and more conscious. Conscious past life memories are increasing. Stories like this are emerging everywhere; a lady visited the ruins of a castle in the UK and as she looked in through the entrance she saw the events that took place in the castle centuries ago as if she had stepped into a movie.

We are beginning to become more conscious in other areas also. All through the day we do, say and think many, many things. Of course we are aware of these things but are we fully aware of all the implications? Sure we see the smile on the face of the person who experiences our good deeds, or scowl for the bad deeds, but that is only half the story.

Every good deed creates warmth in the cosmos. Every loving, thoughtful deed creates warmth which radiates to the Hierarchies and souls in the spiritual worlds. Bright luminous rays result from our good and creative actions. Darkness and cold result from selfish, harmful deeds and thoughts.

So even though we are usually aware of our actions, and the response it brings, this is not the complete story. Every night when we sleep we take these deeds, our words and our thoughts into the spiritual worlds and at the same time they are stored in our semi-conscious levels. The one who is connecting up with their I AM becomes more conscious that their experiences are incomplete, that there is another side to their deeds; they feel maimed, as if a hand or an eye were removed. It is painful. So ordinary life cheats us of the full experience and we bear this as pain.

When people talk about the wing beat of a butterfly causing a storm somewhere, never mind about something happening on the other side of the world, what about striving to become aware of the full effects of each and every act, word and even thought in our own life.

It is when we die, as we stand in our I AMness, that we experience the other side of our deeds. The beings of the Hierarchies look on our earthly actions and we experience, like spiritual rain, their like and dislike for our words, thoughts and deeds. All our goodness is illuminated by the sympathies of these lofty beings and deposited into the communal cosmic bank. Antipathies of the Hierarchies for any of our deeds fill us with a deep urge to grasp them to ourselves so that they do not contaminate the universe. So our destiny, our karma arises from our deep sense of responsibility for the cosmos. We know that our next incarnation will be the opportunity to put it right.

So then it does seem strange that we should squeal and complain about the difficulties life presents – we have chosen them out of our deep sense of responsibility for the Cosmos.

Another thing that is becoming more conscious is the true nature of our I AMness. The I AM that we express each day is really the I AM that we developed in our last life. Do you sometimes feel that you fall short of your potential? Or think that others do? Do you sometimes wonder why others don't see who you really are? This stems from the fact that your "I", which is the sum total of all your past lives, expresses itself to the point that you got to when you last died. The I AM you are continuing to develop now is still in-the-making and won't be expressed in its fullness till your next incarnation. But we can feel this resurrection – "I AM the resurrection" – within us now as a reality. This is why the more Christ enters our life, the more conscious we become and we can begin to express more of our I AM now. "he who believes in me[the I am], though he die, yet shall he live,".

Based on ideas from "*Anthroposophy and the Inner Life.*" Lecture 8, Feb 9 1924

◆

Five: Christ Speaks to Us

Now when Jesus came, he found that Laz'arus had already been in the tomb four days. Bethany was near Jerusalem, about two miles off, and many of the Jews had come to Martha and Mary to console them concerning their brother. When Martha heard that Jesus was coming, she went and met him, while Mary sat in the house. Martha said to Jesus, "Lord, if you had been here, my brother would not have died. And even now I know that whatever you ask from God, God will give you." Jesus said to her, "Your brother will rise again." Martha said to him, "I know that he will rise again in the resurrection at the last day." Jesus said to her, "I am the resurrection and the life; he who believes in me, though he die, yet shall he live, and whoever lives and believes in me shall never die. Do you believe this?" John11:17-26 Read the whole story to verse 44

Our I AM, like Lazarus, is as good as dead, hidden in the cave of our body, veiled by our lack of consciousness. Martha and Mary believe that Lazarus is dead, and that too much time has elapsed for him to be revived, even by the Teacher.

It is interesting that Jesus is referred to as the Teacher. The last reflection spoke of knowledge as the tool to make us conscious. Knowledge is I AM food and love is I AM substance. Such tenderness and love is expressed in those words "Jesus wept." Rudolf Steiner says that it was not for sorrow but for joy that Jesus wept. He wept for joy that the god in Lazarus may be manifest, that the I AM in him may be revealed.

So we work at becoming more and more conscious. We can do this in many, many ways. There is no one way for everyone, there are many paths up the mountain. And thank God for that, if we were all on one path it would be pretty crowded. Wherever the path, and wherever we are on it, we have a companion. Christ is there where we are. We don't have to be somewhere out 'there' where he is said to be. "I am with you always," he said at the end of St Matthew's Gospel, "to the close of the age."

Mary and Martha said *"Lord, if you had been here,"* – they didn't realize the new way Christ is with us now. Now we can see Christ standing before us, speaking personally to us the words so wonderfully preserved in the Bible. "I am with you", "Peace be with you." "Let not your hearts be troubled, neither be afraid."

They are his words and he is speaking them personally to us. We can experience an inner quickening when we hear the words in our Imagination. We can feel a sense of being able to handle anything knowing that Christ is "always with you". The more we make this a reality in our lives the easier it will be to call them to mind when we most need them.

As we live in our tomb, that is, our body, we must become more and more aware that Christ is always on his way to the tomb. He doesn't rush, four days Lazarus has been dead, so this is the fifth day, the fifth epoch in which we now live. Christ is on his way to raise us up, to revive us. Can we hear him say those words to us? *"Lazarus, come out."*

Can we hear him calling to our I AM? It says, *"he cried with a loud voice"*. This is not the still small voice but a loud voice. The voice is not just calling, it says *"he cried"*. We can use our Imagination to hear this voice. Our I AM is entombed and in bondage until we hear it.

The facts are these: we are in this world, we are dead and we are in the tomb of our physical body. We live in a society constructed of dead, material concepts. Therefore society is also a tomb. The whole earth is a tomb too; it is the body of Christ and he is entombed in it waiting for each person to enable his resurrection. Therefore, the more of us that recognize his presence, the more he can enliven the etheric of this world.

Then more and more people will hear him say, *"come out!"* Then we read. *"The dead man came out, his hands and feet bound with bandages, and his face wrapped with a cloth. Jesus said to them, 'Unbind him, and let him go.'"*

If his hands and feet were bound he must have floated out. Jesus didn't say to people, "Go in and carry him out." He cried directly to a dead man whose hands and feet are tied up and whose face is wrapped in a cloth, *"Come out."* We can look at Lazarus in our imagination, constrained like that, and see that his body is actually shaped like the letter "I".

Jesus would not have asked people to help him for the I AM is about freedom. The person who is expressing their I AM doesn't depend on other people. Even though constrained, the I AM can only act in freedom.

These are the thoughts what set us free from the tomb and help us to unbind ourselves. We don't need to strain against the things that bind us; we just need to hear the voice of Christ saying. "Peace be with you". We don't need to cower in the tomb; we just need to hear the voice of Christ crying. "Come out."

Jesus said to her, "I am the resurrection and the life; he who believes in me, though he die, yet shall he live, and whoever lives and believes in me shall never die. Do you believe this?" John 11:25

◆

6. I AM THE WAY, THE TRUTH AND THE LIFE

One: The Way; the Will, the Father

Jesus said to him, "I am the way, and the truth, and the life; no one comes to the Father, but by me. If you had known me, you would have known my Father also; henceforth you know him and have seen him." John14:6f

"I am the way", the word 'way' in the Greek is 'odos', it means the natural way, the way to go. Metaphorically it is a course of conduct and way of thinking.

A 'way' always has a destination and this time the destination is the Father. Not the father Abraham that the Jews spoke of at the time of Christ but God the Father, the originator of the I AM.

In these words, "the way, the truth and the life" dwells the Trinity; Father, Son and Holy Spirit. The 'way' is the Father and requires the will; the 'truth' is Christ the Son which requires thinking; and the Holy Spirit is the 'life'-giving spirit that is felt. Willing, thinking and feeling are the tools which the I AM uses to spiritualize that which has become too earthly, too physical and too instinctual.

It is Thomas who is asking "how can we know the way?" The same Thomas who wanted physical proof, not just to see Jesus' wounds but to put his hands IN them. He is so engrossed in matter that he can't see that the I AM is the 'way'. This 'way' is also the journey of the prodigal son, leaving the father, mucking around with the pigs and then returning to the father.

John the Baptist also impresses on us the importance of the 'way'; "I am the voice of one crying in the wilderness 'Make straight the way of the Lord,' as the prophet Isaiah said." John 1:23

We are, of course, in this wilderness - the solitude - cut off from the spiritual worlds and we are groping to find the 'way'. We are blind and our consciousness is dull. The way stretches out ahead of us but it also stretches back to the past. In our blindness we think that the way stretching back to the past is much safer than the one ahead. After all, it is familiar territory for it is the way we came.

If only we had the courage to trust the way ahead; the I AM is the way ahead "no one comes to the Father, but by (me) the I AM." This 'way' is the way of freedom. We simply decide in the full clear light of consciousness to take this 'way'. It is a free action which is made out of the I AM to take the way forward to the Father, not retrace our steps back to the primal Father. Not to take the way back to the Garden of Eden but forward to the New Jerusalem.

Even though we only have a tentative relationship with the I AM we do know that it is a reality. We know that when we say "I" we can only mean ourselves. If we hear someone else say "I" we know that they are not meaning us. So when we say "I" essentially we name ourselves from within ourselves. This is our inner world and so the "I" - the 'God' within us begins to speak.

We haven't always been able to call ourselves by this sacred name "I". Not so long ago, a few thousand years, we would have literally fainted if we even heard the name "I", we certainly didn't refer to ourselves as "I". Before Golgotha, before Christ united with the earth, only the initiates knew and used the sacred name "I". Since Golgotha not only do we have an increasingly intimate relationship with our I AM, we have the opportunity to Christen our I AM. In fact not to Christen your I AM leads to greater isolation. Christ in you, the hope of glory means Christ is IN us, in our inner being. This is the 'way' now, I AM is the way.

While we learn to engage fully with our I AM, this real self, it is kept for us by our guardian Angel. Rudolf Steiner in lectures to the first Waldorf teachers in 1919 said something surprising: "What do most modern people mean when they say "God"? What kind of being do they refer to when they speak of God? What they mean is an Angel, their own Angel, which they call God! This is only how far we have come along the way since Golgotha." So not until we take our I AM into ourselves can we see past the Angel to God the Father.

When we unite with our I AM, the God within us, then we can know the Father, not before. "If you had known the I AM, you would have known the I AM's Father also; henceforth you know him and have seen him."

It is in our Christed I AM that we also find the 'way' to look at the past, at the 'way' we have conquered and prevailed. We see that when we may have been angry, distressed, sad etc. that now through I AM-infused eyes we have a new way of looking at these character-building episodes.

Then we come near to the glorious point of "Not I but Christ in me."

◆

Two: The Truth; Thinking and Christ

Read John 14:5-21 Jesus said to him (Thomas), "I am the way, and the truth, and the life; no one comes to the Father, but by me. If you had known me, you would have known my Father also; henceforth you know him and have seen him." John14:6-7

"I am the truth" – the Greek word for truth used here is 'aletheia' which indicates the reality lying at the basis of an appearance, the essence of a matter. The I AM is not open to interpretation, it is the naked essence of our being. There can be no pretense; pretense comes from the astral.

The I AM is actually a frightening thing just as the naked truth can be hard to bear. How often do we shrink from truth? John chose to mention this in chapter 16 when he recorded Jesus' words, "I have yet many things to say to you, but you cannot bear them now. John 16:12

Thomas' question: "Where are you going; how can we know the way?" seems to get such an odd answer unless we look at it differently. Esoterically, the Way relates to the Father, and the will; the Truth points to the Son, and to thinking.

In Thomas we see our lost ability to think purely. Knowledge has become abstract and personal and is therefore subjective; our own ideas can stand in the way of truth.

What is thinking really? Thinking is nothing more than placing one concept next to another, one image next to another and by comparing them all we reach a conclusion or make a judgment. Because we are so bound to our physical body, and because our relationship to our I AM is so tentative, most of our concepts and images come from the past. Innately we use the past to understand the present. It is difficult for us to factor in the future when the past is so vivid.

Yet the real purpose of thinking is so that we can understand the reality of our being. The reality of our being is not the past but the future when we will be fully human. The I AM that we are working hard to incorporate into our being has only ever been experienced fully by one man: Jesus. Rev. Mario Schoenmaker would sometimes end his prayers by saying, "We pray these things in the matchless name of Jesus."

What we need is a living thinking, a thinking that can factor in the future. It is only with this kind of living thinking - which uses the etheric body - that we can grasp many of the truths in the Bible. So many biblical statements seem to have little meaning to our earthly mind. Sometimes they even seem to be mindless repetition, or even contradiction. If you had known me, you would have known my Father also; henceforth you know him and have seen him." If we know the I AM then we know the Father, the originator of the I AM. This is like seeing the likeness of the father in his son.

"Believe" says Jesus, not blindly but trust. "Believe me that I am in the Father and the Father in me; or else believe me for the sake of the works themselves." This is not about persuasion, we are asked to take it as fact. We can do this by experiencing thinking as a creative act. When we think we create a form in the astral world. On Old Saturn when the Archai, the time spirits, thought they created a physical form. If we can free our thinking from our nervous system we have creative Imagination. This is thinking that is freed from the brain, it is pure thinking, free thinking. Pure thinking enables us to trust these words and experience the truth that sets us free.

It seems slightly peculiar that Jesus goes on and on about "knowing" except if we understand then that truth speaks about knowing. "I am the truth" tells us that when our I AM is fully engaged we will know. We will know Christ, we will know the Father and we will know the way. Verse 17 says that the Spirit of truth will be revealed to us if we seek it. So we are asked to believe and know and our I AM will be revealed.

Chapter 14 is really quite astounding. Perhaps we should read it as a mantra every morning.

* We will do greater works than Jesus when his fully Christened I AM reconnects with the Father.

* Whatever we ask in the I AM, it will be done.

* Christ will come to us and the comforter/counselor will be sent to abide with us forever.

How could we ever get depressed, anxious or fearful knowing this and believing this? Feel verse 18 reverberate through you.

"I will not leave you desolate; I will come to you. Yet a little while, and the world will see me no more, but you will see me; because I live, you will live also.

♦

Three: The Life; Feeling and the Holy Spirit.

Jesus said to him, "I am the way, and the truth, and the life; no one comes to the Father, but by me. If you had known me, you would have known my Father also; henceforth you know him and have seen him." John14:6f

We have reached the third prong of this I AM saying; I am the life. There are several words for "life" in the Greek language; this one is zoe. It means the living being, the life force. We would call this force the etheric, yet it is more than etheric; it is our purified etheric which we can call Buddhi or Life Spirit. It is the I AM infused etheric force. This etheric is raised up and spiritualized so that it becomes a living force not bound to the physical. Such a living force overcomes death and the deadly ways of this world.

It is interesting to note that the word "life" is used in all the I AM sayings except the last one; but "I am the vine" speaks about the life source. The fourth I AM saying about the Good Shepherd who lays down his life uses a different word for 'life', Psuche which means soul. These are the ways John uses the word life:

1. the bread of life (zoe) 2. the light of life 3. I came that they may have life, 4. The good shepherd lays down his life (psuche) for the sheep. 5. I am the resurrection and the life 6. I am the way, the truth and the life 7. I am the true vine – (the vine is the life source)

Another word for life is pneuma and this word speaks of the Holy Spirit or the holy breath. Since we have been comparing the 'way' (Father - will) the 'truth' (Son - thinking) and the 'life' to the Trinity; the 'life' then is the Holy Spirit and feeling.

Now the Holy Spirit is the Counselor and John 14 tells us twice about the Counselor.

On verse 16 "And I will pray the Father, and he will give you another Counselor, to be with you for ever", and then 10 verses later – "But the Counselor, the Holy Spirit, whom the Father will send in my name, he will teach you all things, and bring to your remembrance all that I have said to you."

As we contemplate these ideas we must be aware that we are death beings; the life of our physical body depends on destruction, we kill nature to nourish our body, we kill the oxygen that we breathe and so on. This life that consumes and depletes is "bios" and is related to our body, zoe is about the life of our spirit. Zoe is the life that does not experience death, it is eternal. The I AM is all about eternity. Eternity is not in the far distant future, eternity simply means not to have boundaries. It is the present free of the boundaries of the physical, sense world. That's what "I am the life" says to us.

While we are trying to experience the reality of this eternity we have the counselor "to be with you for ever." And to "to teach you all things, including the things you have forgotten."

What have we forgotten? The highest initiate who incarnates again as a tiny baby forgets everything. It is interesting to consider Steiner saying that the shepherds and the disciples were high initiates. However, because consciousness had evolved since they were initiates they had to start again. This is reminiscent of the temple steps. Each initiation at each stage of evolution is another step closer to the temple of God. The initiate is always at the forefront of evolution. Today we are no longer in the temple but in modern everyday life striving to evolve our consciousness to the highest possible state for our time. It wouldn't be right to express the consciousness of another era today; that would be dragging the past into the present which always bears the stamp of Lucifer.

Rev Mario Schoenmaker, in his discourses on the Gospel of St Mark, spoke about this also. He said that children often have a major illness around the turn of the seven year cycles. They may lose consciousness for about 3 days – like the temple sleep – in this way they re-experience something of their past initiations. It is as if they are catching up with themselves and can then further develop their consciousness in the current life.

Initiation is not such a mysterious process; it is the integration of our I AM. It means that we are able to pass through the door from earthly life to spiritual life. In the third I AM saying: I am the Door – Christ says, "I (the I AM) came that they may have life, and have it abundantly."

These are great gifts that are placed within our reach. All we have to do is to see the giver as he stands before us in his etheric presence. He gave us the symbols of bread and wine so that we could experience the reality of his abundant life. Religious feelings are the greatest life-giver to the etheric body. When our consciousness awakens through the power of the I AM the elements of the communion take on new meaning. The bread becomes our brain and the wine becomes our heart; they become Christ's substance and essence. Our task is to join the head and the heart; we place the bread in the wine within us so that the lower is conquered and raised up and we know and see the Father.

◆

Four: The Inner Law of the I AM is Grace

Read John 13:36 – 14:8 Jesus said to him, "I am the way, and the truth, and the life; no one comes to the Father, but by me. If you had known me, you would have known my Father also; henceforth you know him and have seen him." John14:6f

This I AM saying is sandwiched between Thomas and Philip speaking about deeply spiritual things from a material, earthly point of view. How can we find the way and how will we recognize the Father? - as if the way is a road and Father is man they will encounter on the road.

These disciples were steeped in the laws that were necessary to bring Christ to earth; they didn't see that the laws had passed their use-by date. We are in the same position as we forge a closer relationship with our I AM and with Christ. The laws of this world cast a veil over the way.

Even before Thomas spoke, Peter had eagerly offered to lay down his life to follow Christ - now! (much easier than finding his own way later he probably thought). This too is our challenge. To lay down our life is to stop operating through that part of our etheric force which is saturated with matter, which is influenced by earthly concerns and the law (karma). Christ said "I have power to lay it (life) down, and I have power to take it again;" The question is: How can we lay down our earthly etheric force and take up our Life Spirit; the raised, spiritualized etheric forces?

It cannot be done through rules and regulations and having others lording over us. Grace has replaced the law. Grace is the awakening of the I AM which needs no law, no external regulation. Grace is the inner law given to those who have been freed in Christ. Now external authority becomes internal responsibility … one comedian cleverly calls it 'response-a-liberty.' We have been given self-governance, not to do as we like but through Grace to do the good.

This I AM saying tells us about a process that we are living through now. Christ is etherically present and we are continually looking for the way to see him in a world that is spiralling into abstraction and so-called truth is nothing but smoke and mirrors. Life is only seen in terms of a physical body; post-death and pre-birth are not familiar concepts. The law is an ass; the innocent are jailed while the guilty roam free.

Those with esoteric understanding have the great consolation that the inner law, Grace, cannot be violated. It stands in its purity. It is a gift but it cannot be unwrapped until the giver is received. Over this sacred privilege presides the Comforter.

John tells us that "he will teach you all things, and bring to your remembrance all that he has said to you."

In our effort to allow our I AM more influence in our daily affairs, and to include Christ in the process, and concurrently spiritualize our etheric forces, we will remember. When we experience this remembrance we will need comforting. Why? Because we will remember our past lives. We will remember all our deaths, the way we died; and the way we caused others to die. We will see where we have strayed from our blueprint. We will become more and more conscious of the way our past deeds influence our present life. We will see how we must make conscious choices to create the right future. Only if the Christ Impulse is awakened in us will we be able to view all this objectively. Objectivity does not mean in a disassociated way. We will be able to experience it fully but through different eyes; "full of grace and truth". This is the Grace given to us by Christ.

So the way to our Real Self means that we have to loosen our etheric, tame our astral and see the risen Christ. The problem is that our etheric likes the memories of the good old days and our astral loves our old consciousness full of our passions and desires. This makes it very hard to stand in our I AM and express all the talents and gifts we have accrued over lifetimes. If we accept that the Comforter is at our side then we have the courage to leave the old ways and dare to stand in our I AM. Then we stand in the present while embracing the future. Then we will begin to use the gift of Grace that is ours, and our talents which are hidden in our I AM will come to the fore. Then we can truly say that we are gifted. And we say that talented people are gifted don't we. To be gifted is to have Grace. With St Paul we can say, "I can do all things in him (the Lord, the I AM) who strengthens me."

♦

7. I AM THE TRUE VINE

One: Taking Responsibility

"I am the true vine, and my Father is the vinedresser. Every branch of mine that bears no fruit, he takes away, and every branch that does bear fruit he prunes, that it may bear more fruit. You are already made clean by the word which I have spoken to you. Abide in me, and I in you. As the branch cannot bear fruit by itself, unless it abides in the vine, neither can you, unless you abide in me. I am the vine, you are the branches. He who abides in me, and I in him, he it is that bears much fruit, for apart from me you can do nothing. If a man does not abide in me, he is cast forth as a branch and withers; and the branches are gathered, thrown into the fire and burned. John 15:1-6

How interesting that the first I AM saying is about bread, the last one is about wine.

The I AM is the vine that supports the results of our work. If the I AM tries to grow without involving Christ, for a while its branches will look healthy but then they will wither. Other branches will look promising and then bear no fruit. Each branch could be seen as a task; to love, to create, to gain wisdom, to be disciplined, to be objective, to resist being judgmental, to respect, to be thoughtful, to see and do the good. The list is endless.

Imagine this vine; see it roots in the earth drawing up the

minerals and moisture from the soil; the soil which is now the substance of the body of Christ and the water which is the blood of Christ. How strong and supple is the vine? Move up the vine in your imagination and see the leaves, some are tender and green, others are old and weathered. Some have a spot of mold which results from opposition to the life force in the vine.

If, in a moment of ecstasy, we say to the Vinedresser, "not your will but thine" and the next day exert our own will, or worse exert our will onto others, a branch will wither.

Let's say that our financial situation is causing anxiety. We look for ways to improve it but nothing seems to work and our anxiety rises. Our branch will wither or it won't produce fruit until we are able to see that whatever we experience in life is exactly what we are meant to experience. That it is the will of the Father. Then even if we manage to accept the situation without one twinge of anxiety, just to make absolutely sure that we are a strong fruit-producing branch, the Vinedresser lops off our effort. This is the real test. Can we stand in our I AM knowing that we can do all things only in him - in Christ – who strengthens us. Php 4:13

My heart aches when I see the children in Middle East, their little faces in agony, hardly able to cry for the horror they see - as if they know that their tears will achieve nothing. It is a picture of innocence violated. But isn't it also the picture of the Vinedresser pruning? If they can bear it, if they can stand in the midst of the craziness, their I AM will prevail over the group consciousness that infiltrates their existence. Christ appears to those who are scourged and prevail because they become one with him.

Imagine the vine again. See the tendrils, reaching into the air until they find something solid to curl around. Are they strong, are they supporting the vine as it grows to reach the sunlight? Are they strong enough to withstand the winds that blow in many distractions?

Do we support ourselves or are we always looking outside ourselves for support? Do we stand in our I AM and accept responsibility for all that comes our way? Often we don't, we look outside ourselves because we are used to the support of old gods. We are still getting used to the god within which supports us through our own efforts.

Now look to the branches with their tiny buds of fruit. This fruit is the result of the I AM which is grounded in Christ. If this fruit is the result of the pseudo I AM, the astral; the seat of do-goodery, pride, selfishness and thoughtlessness, then the branch will bear no fruit. If we are oblivious to our environment or parochial or harbor feelings of jealousy, guilt etc. we will be gathered up and burned. We must be purified of all these things if the I AM is to be the vine that meets the Vinedresser's standards.

We have been given the I AM and the way it develops depends entirely on our own work. The sooner we accept that, the sooner we will be at peace. "I am the vine, you are the branches. He who abides in me, and I in him, he it is that bears much fruit".

◆

Two: Thinking Under Control

"I am the true vine, and my Father is the vinedresser. Every branch of mine that bears no fruit, he takes away, and every branch that does bear fruit he prunes, that it may bear more fruit. You are already made clean by the word which I have spoken to you. Abide in me, and I in you. As the branch cannot bear fruit by itself, unless it abides in the vine, neither can you, unless you abide in me. I am the vine, you are the branches. He who abides in me, and I in him, he it is that bears much fruit, for apart from me you can do nothing. If a man does not abide in me, he is cast forth as a branch and withers; and the branches are gathered, thrown into the fire and burned. John 15:1-6

The I AM is the vine, the branches and fruit represent our work. Given that the I AM is primarily expressed in thinking these branches can represent our thoughts. Are our thoughts fruitful or are they withered? Fruitful thoughts would be full of courage and boldness. They would honest and open. They would embrace the future and all that is new, they would be creative, productive and uplifting.

Withered thoughts are negative. They would be the thoughts of not being good enough, of not being able to achieve, of not being worthy. On the other hand they could be the thoughts that overestimate our ability. Or they could be thoughts that continually revisit bad experiences preventing us from moving on. They would also thoughts that are judgmental of others; premature thoughts that under value others. They can also be our abstract thoughts or anxious thoughts.

Rev Mario Schoenmaker often stressed the need to be in charge of our thinking. Thinking must be clear and objective he often said. Can we control our thoughts? When a destructive thought begins to form in our soul how soon can we nip it in the bud? Thinking is a tool of the I AM and the more our I AM can use this tool, the more controlled our thinking will be.

Thinking is not simply the product of our brain as we are led to believe. Thinking is a spiritual element that we take into ourselves. If we drink water we don't say that the water came out of our tongue do we? Nor do our thoughts come out of our brain; the brain and its nerves are the conduit for our thoughts.

This flow of thoughts can be conscious or unconscious. The unconscious flow of thoughts belongs to an ancient consciousness, we could call it psychism. The conscious flow of thoughts belongs to the new human consciousness which we can call clairvoyance – clear seeing.

"Every time you have a thought, as it is happening in your brain, it is also happening in the Cosmos," says Rev Mario Schoenmaker in his lectures on the Book of Hebrews (Lecture 32). He explains that when we can really experience thinking as a cosmic rather than a personal event we assist Christ and become co-creators with Christ. Then, through our effort, the deterioration of thinking in the world is reversed. What a huge responsibility!

If we take this seriously the first thing we realize is that our thinking is no longer private and personal. What we think is everybody's business because what we think affects the whole Cosmos. This is why Christ is telling us that the I AM is the vine and the Father is standing by with the secateurs.

Thinking is an extraordinary resource. Rev Mario Schoenmaker regularly said that we have to see spirit in every manifested thing. If we can't see spirit in all that meets our eye; the other person, or the food we are eating, etc. then think it! With our thinking we can remind ourselves that the world around us is pulsating with spiritual beings shaping and forming physical matter. Each day we can try to make a point of thinking to ourselves when we look at a flower, "the shape, the color, the smell of this flower is the result of the activity of spiritual beings". When that experience becomes real to us we are filled with awe.

Those who are serious about controlling their thoughts can set aside five minutes each day to think about one particular object; a needle or a pencil. Goethe did this for hours at a time and then he came to the idea of the Ur-plant. Hold the pencil in your mind and think about its shape, its length, its lead, think about how it is made. Think as many thoughts about the pencil as you can but do not allow any other thoughts in. When another thought intrudes use your will to remove it. It is the will that can control thoughts. If you can hold the pencil easily in your thoughts for five minutes then try to do it for ten minutes. In this way we can strengthen our will. Then we will give life to our dead thinking though our own efforts and we will be a co-creator with Christ – abiding in him and he in us.

♦

Three: Feelings Under Control

"I am the true vine, and my Father is the vinedresser. Every branch of mine that bears no fruit, he takes away, and every branch that does bear fruit he prunes, that it may bear more fruit. You are already made clean by the word which I have spoken to you. Abide in me, and I in you. As the branch cannot bear fruit by itself, unless it abides in the vine, neither can you, unless you abide in me. I am the vine, you are the branches. He who abides in me, and I in him, he it is that bears much fruit, for apart from me you can do nothing. If a man does not abide in me, he is cast forth as a branch and withers; and the branches are gathered, thrown into the fire and burned." John 15:1-6

Last time we identified our thoughts as the branches and fruit of the vine, now let's have a look at feelings or emotions in the same way. Feelings arise in the astral levels of our being. These feelings which we can experience as very strong forces, are mostly only semi-conscious. This is why they can rise up and overwhelm us at times when we are less vigilant. At the core of our feeling levels we find our likes and dislikes; they are powerful forces which must increasingly come under the control of our I AM. If the feeling levels are to be useful for our development they must abide in the I AM and the I AM in them.

One important function of our feelings is when they enliven our hard, cold thoughts. Thinking that is not infused with feeling is abstract and irrelevant in the spiritual scheme of things and will be thrown into the fire.

Of the three soul functions we have the closest affinity to feelings; we are far more comfortable with feelings than we are with thinking and willing. Feeling something requires much less effort than thinking about something or acting out of our own will. Yet we can get into the most trouble with our feelings if they are left to their own devices.

The instinctive level of feelings is to put self first. How will it affect me? How do I feel about that? It is only afterwards that we consider the other person's position. "I am hot, let's open the windows." "I am hungry let's eat." Mothers and lovers would be the only ones who automatically think of the other person first. If our feelings can become more conscious we will be thoughtful of others. When feelings are dominated by our astral rather than our I

AM we will always put ourselves first.

Notice how conversations can be so self-centered. If we mention something we are working on, say writing a book, one response might be, "I'm not reading much at the moment." It is our feelings which prevent us from staying with the other person and sharing their experience as fully as possible. We retreat too soon into ourselves and express our position, we use the barometer of our own semi-conscious feelings. But Christ says *"He who abides in me, and I in him, he it is that bears much fruit,"*

There are a few easy ways to ennoble our feeling levels. One is appreciation of the arts and the other one is to experience religion – not necessarily in a modern church, but to have a genuine experience of the living Christ. The word religion means "to bind" and feelings are like the icing in the biscuit of thinking and willing.

Our etheric body, which has retracted into our physical body, is re-emerging out of the body at this point in evolution. For the etheric to emerge in the right way our thinking must be softened by feeling. Those who look to science rather than Christ as the foundation of the world will experience great anxiety, great nervous agitation.

Religious impulses filled with the etheric presence of Christ work on our etheric body so that part of it is raised out of our body and transformed, spiritualized into Buddhi, Life Spirit or Logos. *"You are already made clean by the word (logos) which I have spoken to you. Abide in me, and I in you." Vs 3&4*

The importance of abiding in the other is stressed over and over. Abide in the I AM instead of in our lower self-centered levels. Abide in the other person; experience their situation as if it were our own. If we can discipline feelings we will transform our astral into Spirit Self. The catch-cry today to 'express yourself' is a ploy by the anti-forces to stop us from spiritualizing ourselves. We mustn't express our feelings indiscriminately, we must discipline them. When we do this we strengthen ourselves. Expressed emotions often deplete us of our energy. When we become more conscious of our feeling levels the more we will be aware of the etheric Christ as he stands in our midst.

◆

Four: Willing Under Control

"I am the true vine, and my Father is the vinedresser. Every branch of mine that bears no fruit, he takes away, and every branch that does bear fruit he prunes, that it may bear more fruit. You are already made clean by the word which I have spoken to you. Abide in me, and I in you. As the branch cannot bear fruit by itself, unless it abides in the vine, neither can you, unless you abide in me. I am the vine, you are the branches. He who abides in me, and I in him, he it is that bears much fruit, for apart from me you can do nothing. If a man does not abide in me, he is cast forth as a branch and withers; and the branches are gathered, thrown into the fire and burned." John 15:1-6

This final reflection on the I AM sayings comes four days before Michaelmas: the festival of will-filled thinking. The ultimate expression of the I AM is will-filled thinking infused with Christened feeling.

We can look at the vine's branches now as the will. Will is a mysterious force within us. At the foundation of the processes of our physical body lies the unconscious will. It is through the will that we survive as a physical being. If we had to remember to breathe every few seconds we would have died long ago. If we had to consciously digest our food, oxygenate our blood, move fluids around our body etc. we would not last very long.

Will can also be identified as that impulse of warmth which develops into motivation; the will to do a thing. It rises up as inner initiative. This means that the will is also about freedom and this fact links it to the I AM for the hallmark of the I AM is freedom. So there are two sides to the will; a side which is unconscious and by it we survive in the physical world and the other side which can be exercised in full freedom.

We often use our will in a withered way. One of these is when we judge others – we impose our will on them. Judgment must always be suspended until we are aware of twelve sides of a situation.

If we become engrossed in an annoyance then our will is withered. The differences we experience in our relationships are the grit that creates the pearl of our being, which is our I AM. It is not about feeling the annoyance, but resisting it. Furthermore, the thing that annoys us in the other person is often something that annoys us in ourselves. The strong I AM always seeks to be objective. The strong I AM lives in freedom and grants others the freedom to be. There is an excellent quote about this, "A friend is someone who won't allow you to be anyone other than yourself."

There are many philosophies that encourage people to tackle their difficulties by examining them in the hope of conquering them. This is very hard work and success can be illusive. Rev Mario Schoenmaker used to say that the only way to conquer our less satisfactory aspects was to hose them out and focus only of our I AM and Christ.

The only way to do this is to acquaint ourselves with our I AM. How and when do we express our I AM? Primarily through our posture and our movement, through our speech and through our thinking. By becoming more aware of our expression in these three areas we will increase our awareness of our I AM. Then the I AM will have a greater influence in these ways;

- in our will influencing our movement and action,

- in our feeling in our use of words and tone of voice,

- and in our thinking which will become clear and pure.

As our connection with our I AM grows then the light of Christ will irradiate our I AM and we will hear Christ speak these intimate words to us: *Abide in me and I in you.*

Then we hear the great promise, *"If you abide in me, and my words abide in you, ask whatever you will, and it shall be done for you."*

If we abide in the I AM and the I AM's words (not *logos* here but *rhema* which indicates speech) abide in us, ask whatever we wish (is the real meaning of the word 'will' here). The secret about wishing is that it is fulfilled in the future. So we are told here the esoteric secret that we can determine our future incarnations. This is the true purpose of the will, the freedom to determine our future.

Six months before Rev Mario Schoenmaker died he prayed this beautiful prayer which reveals much about our I AM

O Lord, God of the Universe,
revealed in our innermost being,

- which makes us cosmic beings -
reveal yourself more deeply through us;
make our I AM alive with the flow of your spirit,
with the fullness of your love.
And may we who are your offspring, God-beings,
live in this world with joy and peace,
with compassion and creative intent.
May we at all times know that we are united with you
and with all those who consciously know their I AMness.
This we pray in the name of that great I AM,
who walked this earth in completeness,
Jesus Christ, our Lord. So shall it be. Rev Mario Schoenmaker
30 June 1996 (edited)

♦♦♦

RESOURCES

Print publications

I Connecting : The Soul's Quest ISBN 978-0-9779825-3-0
www.i-connecting.com published by Goldenstone Press July 2007
Published as an ebook in Kindle 2012 under the title
I AM The Mystery
Workbook and workshop associated with this work
http://i-connecting.com/Workbook
http://i-connecting.com/Workshop

The Soul's Secret Unveiled in the Book of Revelation I AM The
Soul's Heartbeat. Volume 1 The Seven I AM Sayings in St John's
Gospel: 2003

Reflection series by Kristina Kaine now in Kindle Books.

1. I AM The Soul's Heartbeat. Volume 1
The Seven I AM Sayings in St John's Gospel: 2003

2. I AM The Soul's Heartbeat. Volume 2
Christian Initiation in St John's Gospel: 2003 – 2004

3. I AM The Soul's Heartbeat. Volume 3
Finding the Eightfold Path of Buddha in St John's Gospel: 2004

4. I AM The Soul's Heartbeat. Volume 4
The Twelve Disciples in St John's Gospel: 2005

5. I AM The Soul's Heartbeat. Volume 5
Seven Signs in St John's Gospel: 2006

6. I AM The Soul's Heartbeat. Volume 6
The Beatitudes in St John's Gospel: 2006 – 2007

7. The Soul's Secret Unveiled in the Book of Revelation: 2007 –
2010
2 volumes ebook,1 volume print

8. I AM The Soul's Heartbeat. Volume 7
The Bible Unlocked: 2009 –

9. Who is Jesus : What is Christ : 2010 –

10. I AM Exercises to assist you to become more aware of the
way your I AM interacts with your soul.

References

The Bible, Revised Standard Version

Expository Dictionary of New Testament Words : W. E Vine

Meditation – Guidance of the Inner Life by Friedrich
Rittelmeyer,

Kristina writes regularly about her understanding of the human
soul and spirit. She is an associate director of Spiritual Science
Bible Studies which distributes her weekly Reflections.

You can read more about her at the following websites.
http://www.spiritualsciencebiblestudies.org/
http://www.facebook.com/EsotericConnection
http://www.soulquesting.wordpress.com/
http://www.kristinakaine.posterous.com/
http://www.bibleunlocked.blogspot.com.au/
http://www.esotericconnection.com/
http://www.i-connecting.com/

ABOUT THE AUTHOR

Kristina Kaine has worked with people all her life: during her early career in medical sales and staff recruitment, and for the last 20 years in her own business which matches people in business partnerships, as well as for home sharing and home minding. Through this rich interaction with people, Kristina has observed the struggle for self identity from many angles. She was awakened to the ideas of Rudolf Steiner by Rev Mario Schoenmaker, attending all of Schoenmaker's lectures for 14 years. After Schoenmaker's death in 1997, Kristina realised the need to explain the knowledge of the threefold human being in simple terms that could be applied easily in daily life. As well as her weekly reflections that are read worldwide, she has set this out in her book, 'I Connecting : the Soul's Quest', which was published in 2007 by Robert Sardello. It is not unusual for her to receive comments about her book like this: "It seems like a very lucid treatment, like looking through a clear glass window through which one can discover and recognize the landscape of the soul."